Chicken Little Economics™

Will The Sky Keep Falling?

Edwin K.S. Ryu & Gary Yasumura

CONTENTS

Acknowledgements i

Disclaimer iii

INTRODUCTION 5

CHAPTER ONE: The Long Road to Financial Crisis 7

CHAPTER TWO: How Monetary and Fiscal Policies of Governments Affect You 31

CHAPTER THREE: The Global Debt Crisis 63

CHAPTER FOUR: Looking Ahead: Possible Macroeconomic Scenarios 91

CHAPTER FIVE: Macroeconomic Scenario and Risk Factor Analysis 129

CONCLUSION 143

Resources 147

Endnotes 155

Acknowledgements

We have so many to thank for helping us write this book. Industry associates such as Charles Blankley and Neil Chakerra read key portions of the book and provided useful comments. Arun Chopra was instrumental as a research analyst. Also, many thanks to Betty Matsumoto-Schuch, who designed a great book cover, and to Michelle Hamilton and Angela Fuentes who assisted us with book formatting and interfacing with a subsidiary of Amazon.com, CreateSpace, who helped us self-publish this book. Last, but not least, is Julie Satake Ryu who cooked countless gourmet dinners and remained patient and supportive throughout the long writing process.

Disclaimer

Edwin K.S. Ryu, one of the co-authors, is the principal of Legacy Wealth Advisors, LLC, a wealth management and investment advisory firm.

The views expressed in this book are the authors' own views and not the views of Legacy Wealth Advisors, LLC or any of the institutions Mr. Ryu is affiliated with as a shareholder or Board member.

The information and opinions contained in this document are for information and discussion purposes only, do not constitute a financial promotion and do not purport to be full or complete. While the authors have used their best efforts to ensure the accuracy or completeness of any information contained herein, no reliance may be placed for any purpose on the information or opinions contained in this book or their accuracy or completeness. No representation, warranty or undertaking, express or implied, is given as to the accuracy or completeness of the information or opinions contained in this book and no liability is accepted for the accuracy or completeness of any such information or opinions.

This book does not constitute or form part of any offer to issue or sell, or any solicitation of any offer to subscribe or purchase, any securities or any other interests nor shall it or the fact of its distribution form the basis of, or be relied on in connection with, any contract thereof. In this spirit, no individual securities are discussed within this book. This book is not intended to constitute, and should not be construed to be investment advice. Discussion of investment concepts and principles, such as Modern Portfolio Theory (MPT), is purposely broad in nature and for educational purposes only. You should consult with your investment advisor on any specific investment matters.

INTRODUCTION

"The issue with debt is you can't get rid of it quickly and you can't get rid of it nicely." – Dr. Carmen Reinhart

In these unsettled economic times, all of us wonder whether the sky will keep falling. When we undertook this bookwriting project, our goal was to analyze and understand what happened in 2008-2009. Media business reporters and their guests wax and wane about the latest economic indicators. Lately, optimists point to the signs of economic recovery while "doom and gloomers" continue to compete with the same Pollyannas for headlines. We believe that the massive amounts of United States and global debt, in both the private and government sectors, will likely continue to dampen growth on the economic front. In the advanced economies, the arrival of the 2007-2009 Great Recession abruptly ended a major multi-decade credit expansion that created unprecedented levels of global debt. Many people mistakenly think one or two specific events, such as the mortgage crisis or the use of derivatives, were the culprits behind the Great Recession. In chapters one and two, we set forth our primary belief that the causal factors behind the crisis actually began over a century ago and then intensified and multiplied after the early 1970s. Easy money policies, rampant government spending, and a lax regulatory environment all contributed to the biggest economic bust and financial crisis in a generation. In chapters three and four, we explain the depth, shape and the possible consequences of the global debt crisis, present different economic scenarios for the United States that could transpire and the effect of each one on the dollar, employment and other concerns. Through the course of the book, we examine other advanced economies, including Japan and those in Europe, where we see elevated levels of debt accumulation. The unwinding of global debt will likely have significant, long term repercussions affecting all of us.

No one knows definitively where the world economy is headed or what investments are going to succeed in the future. In "The Fortune Sellers: The Big Business of Buying and Selling Predictions," Brandeis Professor William Sherden studied decades of leading forecasters' proclamations for accuracy. Sherden wrote, "In fact, these experts whose advice we pay handsomely for routinely fail to predict the major events that shape our world, or even the major turning points—the transitions from status quo to something new—whether it be the economy, stock market, weather, or new technologies."[1] We have heeded his conclusions about forecasting and don't profess to own a crystal ball. However, Sherden gave advice about how to extract valuable nuggets of information from the forecasts. In this vein, we have identified and attempted to listen closely to those few economic analysts who correctly foresaw the coming of the Great Recession and financial crash of 2007-2009.

In our closing chapter, the challenging problem of investing during uncertain and volatile macroeconomic times is broached. We believe that the fundamental, core tenants of Modern Portfolio Theory or MPT are still valid. But we believe that an additional component of investing can include economic scenario analysis and planning, which employs a top-down global macro approach to investing. At this point in time, it is more of an art than a science. An investor must understand how one's portfolio may be influenced by economic conditions such as recession, depression, slow growth, hyperinflation or stagflation. A starting point in this process is to identify which asset classes, geographical areas, and long term trends will perform well or poorly in the coming years. How those asset classes and risk factors behave in response to various possible economic scenarios are paramount to building a framework within which one can adjust portfolios by overweighting or underweighting certain asset classes.

Our goal in writing this book is not to recommend how to invest, but to assist you with building a framework within which you can begin the process. Our sincere hope is that economic scenario analysis and planning will be further researched, tested, and validated in the future.

CHAPTER ONE

The Long Road to Financial Crisis

"Yes, Chicken Little, the sky was falling!"

INTRODUCTION

We will endeavor to shed light on the events causing a century of growing debt, inflation and its effects. Each sector of society, corporations, private citizens and government has contributed to overall debt and inflation. During and after the Great Recession, most corporations and private citizens have been deleveraging—that is—attempting to raise capital and/or reduce debt. Governments have been trying to resuscitate slow growth economies by using financial stimuli that tends to increase national debt. In the long run, they may not overcome massive financial markets that often dwarf government budgets. All the trillions of dollars spent on fiscal stimuli and low interest rates may not offset massive private and corporate deleveraging. The slow but inexorable social and economic decision-making force of billions of individuals will eventually move markets in spite of what governments may want or attempt to dictate. As we move beyond the 2008 financial crisis and the Great Recession, some economic analysts are detecting subtle indications that the record breaking global and national debt per GDP may turn disinflation into deflation.

WHAT IS INFLATION?

A low level of price inflation is similar to erosion of a beach. A century ago, your grandfather looked out upon the waves where water meets beach. Each year, although the shoreline moves one foot closer to your beach house, no one is troubled. Your father thinks the ocean is a little closer, but reasons that there is plenty of time and sometimes sand actually piles up rather than disappears. The sun and sand are warm, look inviting and all is well. He forgets to warn you of possible trouble ahead. A hundred years later, you gaze at the shoreline with a disquieting feeling. "What's different?" you ask. After a particularly severe storm, you grimly realize that the ocean is lapping at your property line whereas in your youth it was much farther away.

Inflation is similar in nature. Year after year, little by little, inflation erodes away the purchasing power of your dollars. After this last particularly severe financial crisis, we realize that our dollar has lost over 90% of its buying power in a hundred years as shown by Figure 1-1. Unfortunately many other currencies have experienced similar declines. Inflation's effects are many, and in the long run, can wreak havoc on economies and society.

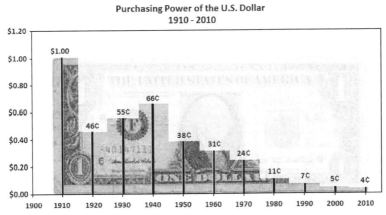

Figure 1-1: Purchasing Power of the U.S. Dollar 1910 - 2010
Source: MeasuringWorth: http://www.measuringworth.com/uscompare/

Before we discuss inflation, we have to agree on its definition. Most people believe inflation consists of rising prices and wages because that affects their lives the most and is directly observable. However price and wage levels are symptoms of inflation; so we start with a definition of inflation by economist Murray Rothbard, who was a proponent of the Austrian school of economics. He defined inflation as an increase in the money supply that, in turn, leads to a nominal price level higher than it would have been without the inflation.[2] In other published works, Rothbard and others maintained that bank credit expansion worsened the inflationary effects of money supply expansion. To reinforce this proposition, we will discuss later on in this chapter how the less-regulated shadow banks generated far more credit expansion than the monetary authorities expanded the money supply. Thus we would define inflation as an increase in the supply of *credit* and money that, in turn, leads to a nominal price level higher than it would have been without the inflation.

The Effect of Credit on Inflation

In a fiat-money and credit-based economic system, credit is often the key to inflation and deflation since credit, especially that being created by the shadow banking system, can dwarf the official money supply. The shadow or "parallel" banks were non-depository, less regulated banks and financial institutions such as investment banks, money market funds, insurance companies, hedge funds or sovereign wealth funds whose assets exceeded those of the traditional commercial banking systems. These largely unregulated shadow banks often had a 30:1 to 60:1 ratio of debt relative to assets. U.S. shadow bank liabilities topped around $20 trillion in 2007 while U.S. commercial bank liabilities were about $10 trillion in 2007.[3]

Those who follow only a nation's money supply, such as the Federal Reserve's monetary aggregates M1, M2 or the Adjusted Monetary Base, may incorrectly forecast high inflation when money supply grows, but credit in the general economy declines. An investigation of the Adjusted Monetary Base, which is the sum total of coins, paper money, and commercial banks' reserves with the Federal Reserve, is revealing. The Federal Reserve Bank partially controls and attempts to influence price levels by using several tools such as the Adjusted Monetary Base.[4] In the latter part of 2008, a credit freeze overtook the global financial system. In an effort to stave off deflation, provide liquidity and increase bank lending, the Federal Reserve Bank increased the Adjusted Monetary Base from $964 billion in September 2008 to $2623 billion at the end of 2011, an increase of 272%. One need only examine Federal Reserve data called "Excess Reserves of Depository Institutions (EXCRESNS)" for the same period. Bank reserves grew from $59.5 billion to $1502.2 billion or a 2400% growth, which shows that the Federal Reserve's attempt to increase lending was disappointing.[5] In addition, shadow bank liabilities decreased from 2008's $19.98 trillion to 2011's $15.3 trillion, a 23.4% decline, which shows how much shadow bank credit decreased.[6] During this same period, the Bureau of Labor Statistics showed the Consumer Price Index rising from only 218.9 to 227.5 or a paltry 3.94% CPI increase.[7]

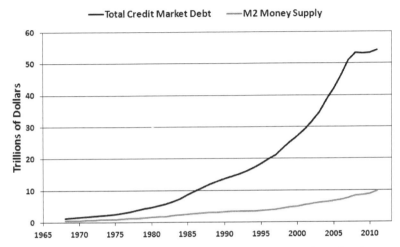

Figure 1-2: Total Credit Market Debt, M2 Money Supply, $ Trillions
Source: Federal Reserve[8]

Remember that one person's credit is another person's debt. Thus when we discuss the growth of credit, it's really the danger of record amounts of debt that concerns us. Richard Duncan is chief economist at Blackhorse Asset Management and author of *The New Depression: The Breakdown of the Paper Money Economy.* Duncan argues convincingly that credit has grown so many times larger than the money supply that money has become far less important in affecting economic activity. The Federal Reserve releases Z.1 Flow of Funds Accounts of the United States providing data for Total Credit Market Debt. In 1968, the United States Total Credit Market Debt was $1.37 trillion. In 2011, it reached $54.1 trillion or an increase of 40 times.[9] This is equivalent to an 8.92% average annual credit growth rate year-over-year for 40 years. In comparison, M2 Money supply in 1968 was $0.59 trillion and in 2011 it was $9.7 trillion, which is an increase of 16.4 times.[10] He believes this credit explosion came about after the

United States halted the requirement for gold to back 25% of our dollars in 1968, liberally relaxed banks' fractional reserve requirements over the years, created many new categories of lenders, invented credit instruments with no reserve requirements at all and foreign entities began supplying the U.S. with 15% of its credit needs.[11] The result has been price and asset inflation and a transformation of our economy from a capitalistic to a credit-oriented economy. Instead of savings and capital driving production and generating wealth, credit creation instigates more debt and consumption.[12]

When discussing inflation, we are referring to price inflation in most instances, but will use the terms price inflation, wage inflation, asset inflation or money supply inflation to distinguish between the different types of inflation when required.

In 2012 as we labor through the aftermath of the Great Recession and its attendant credit contraction, we see the possible glimmerings of deflation in spite of massive government intervention. Disinflation, stagnating or depressed wages and asset deflation are now normal. Why is this happening? The answer lies in the decades-long creation of debt. Our economy is continuing the destruction of vast amounts of credit through deleveraging by corporations, families and individuals. It's happening in spite of rising government debt. Other advanced economies are going through the same experience. We will go into more detail about this phenomenon in the third chapter on debt and credit.

OUR MONEY IS DEBT

Creating Money by Creating Debt

Central banks increase or decrease the money supply by creating or withdrawing credit. Our Federal Reserve Bank attempts to do this by using the "fractional reserve" banking system. Congress has been deficit financing government expenditures for decades by periodically voting to raise the total federal debt ceiling. To cover the Federal government's debt, the U.S. Treasury sells its bills, notes and bonds effectively borrowing money from the public, foreigners or other countries. The Federal Reserve Bank can conduct open market purchases of U.S. Treasury bonds leaving purchasers with cash. When these actions are followed over a long period of time, the effect is to increase the money supply, increase demand for goods, and raise prices and/or wages.[13]

The private commercial banks have been creating most of our money using the fractional reserve banking system. In this practice, the banks hold only a fraction of their deposits as cash or its equivalents and loan out the rest. On William Hummel's website called <u>MONEY WHAT IT IS HOW IT WORKS</u>, commercial banks' method for increasing or decreasing the money supply is explained:

Bank Lending

Banks are not ordinary intermediaries. Like non-banks, they also borrow, but they do not lend the deposits they acquire. They lend by crediting the borrower's account with a new deposit, and then if necessary borrowing the funds needed to meet the reserve ratio requirement. The accounts of other depositors remain intact and their deposits fully available for withdrawal. Thus a bank loan increases the total of bank deposits, which means an increase in the money supply. When the loan is paid off, the money supply decreases.[14]

Under this process, the Federal Reserve Bank cannot necessarily increase the money supply at will, at all times. The Fed can purchase assets directly from the banks creating greater banking reserves, but the banks don't necessarily have to lend them out, which would have increased the money supply. The banks have several likely reasons for not increasing lending to any great extent.

First, they might be afraid of slow economic growth and poor business conditions that makes potential lenders poorer credit risks. Second, because short-term lending rates are so low, the banks can engage in carry trade, the practice of borrowing at low short-term rates and making investments at higher long-term rates. Because the Federal Reserve and other central banks have been forced to keep short-term interest rates low, the banks believe they have a favorable bet on their carry trades. Third, on October 9, 2008, the Fed began paying interest on bank reserves because they thought it would help them control inflation through money supply management. The banks, however, are more likely to hold onto their reserves rather than lending them out since it gives them a risk free albeit small return. Fourth, if deflation appears, their cash reserves become more valuable.[15] Fifth, during the Great Recession and its immediate aftermath, the private sector's demand for loans decreased as businesses deleveraged and watched their markets shrink and individuals also deleveraged while watching their home values dwindle, their income growth rates slow and unemployment rates stay high. Presently even with a tepid recovery, we are still a far cry from where we were before the Great Recession.

Creating Money Out of Nothing

Actual debt monetization occurs when the Federal Reserve Bank creates money ex nihilo, or out of nothing. Only countries that are monetarily sovereign nations can engage in the practice of issuing, withdrawing and controlling their own currency or paper money. Examples of such countries are Japan, United States, Canada, China and Australia. In the United States, its states or municipalities cannot issue their own money. In the European Union's Eurozone, seventeen European nations adopted the Euro and have ceded currency control and issuance to the European Central Bank and are not monetarily sovereign. This principle goes to the core of the problem for highly indebted nations such as Greece, Spain, Italy, Ireland or Portugal. They cannot issue more of their currency or devalue it. A monetarily sovereign currency has a variable exchange rate with respect to other currencies whereas a currency that is pegged or fixed to another currency does not. A monetarily sovereign country such as the United States can set interest rates on its debt instruments and, if they wish, not have to tax or borrow to pay for expenditures. Analysts opine that monetarily sovereign nations can decide not to go bankrupt or default except for political reasons. However there are practical limitations such as too much paper money issuance, which causes high inflation or hyperinflation. Interest rates on government bonds could increase and their prices decline making government deficit financing much more expensive. In addition, other affected nations will try to constrain a money creating nation through currency wars, capital controls or "beggar thy neighbor" policies.[16]

The Fed, with a few computer keystrokes, can create money out of nothing and purchase nearly anything with it such as mortgage backed securities (MBS), stocks, auto loans or commercial paper. When panic gripped the economy and the markets in late 2008 during the Great Recession, this is exactly what the Federal Reserve System began to do. At an unprecedented level, they began lending to troubled banks, provided liquidity to credit starved markets, and began purchasing federal agency debt and mortgage-backed securities (MBSs). The Fed's balance sheet grew from $891 billion in early September 2008 and by early 2013 was over $3 trillion, a 337% increase.[17]

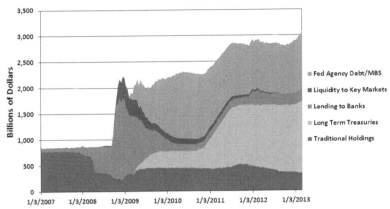

Figure 1-3: Federal Reserve Balance Sheet
Source: Board of Governors of the Federal Reserve System
http://www.federalreserve.gov/releases/h41/,
The Committee for a Responsible Federal Budget
http://stimulus.org/financialresponse/federal-reserve-balance-sheet

THE EROSION OF INFLATION

Ordinary Citizens Always Suffer the Most

Milton Friedman, the Nobel-prize winning economist stated, "Inflation is the one form of taxation that can be imposed without legislation." Inflation weakens a society in many ways. It is one of the main reasons why average workers feel they are no better off or worse off than years ago. Taxpayers begin to understand that price and wage inflation carries them into ever higher tax rate brackets. Retirees who saved diligently all their lives, find that the money they put aside will no longer support them in the manner they had planned as living costs spiral upward. Besides the consequences for individuals, there are other far reaching effects on a national and international level.

The Cycle of Empire, Hegemony, Debt and Inflation

On an international level according to the CIA World FactBook, the United States, Japan, the United Kingdom and other nations, due to decades of debt expansion and monetary inflation, have become the largest debtor nations.[18] History teaches us that debtor nations lose power on the international stage as their economic and military power dwindles. In his bestselling 1987 book, *The Rise and Fall of the Great Powers: Economic Change and Military Conflict from 1500 to 2000*, Professor Paul Kennedy hypothesized that empires or hegemonies gathered great power and influence through economic growth. All great powers will attempt to protect and expand their economic and political interests and/or territories. As Kennedy theorized, they inevitably enlarged and overextended their military forces beyond their ability to finance them. In every instance, as their burgeoning military budgets and economic difficulties grew, its leaders resorted to money supply inflation, currency debasement and/or debt default.[19]

The Roman Empire

We'll investigate even farther back than Kennedy did and study the Roman Empire during the period that historians call the "Crisis of the 3rd Century," which is a textbook example of Professor Kennedy's thesis. Baruch College's Professor Joseph Peden described this period in a lecture titled "Inflation and the Fall of the Roman Empire." The audio recording is available online at: http://media.mises.org/mp3/MoneyandGovernment84/01_1984_Peden.mp3.

The Roman Empire's power and territory grew under Augustus, 31 BC to 14 AD, who added Egypt, northern Spain and large parts of central Europe to the empire. The Roman military and bureaucracy began to grow in size and complexity. Few lands were annexed into Roman rule, but the number of provinces grew from 20 in Augustus' time to 100 provinces in the 3rd century. The 20 provinces had been subdivided over and over to help maintain military control of the subjects. During this 300 year period, the Roman military force expanded from 250,000 to 600,000 men. Emperor Diocletian in 293 A.D. instituted the "Tetrarchy", or "rule of four", wherein each of four emperors administered one fourth of the empire. The Tetrarchy's complexity required four courts, four

Praetorian prefectures, four palaces, and so on. The administrative and military expenses rose massively.[20][21]

Foreign invaders raided the outer provinces. Plague, possibly smallpox, caused many deaths reducing the empire's military capability. The empire broke into civil war as three competing states split from the empire and waged civil war. From 235 to 284 AD, the "Military Anarchy" or "Imperial Crisis" was a period when 20 to 25 mostly Roman generals competed sometimes violently for title of emperor. Each of these emperors had to quickly pay an expensive "accession bonus" to the military. All of these economic and exogenous forces compelled many of the emperors to inflate the currency. They began to debase the empire's coinage, tax estates and capital instead of only income and received taxes in kind. Inflation neared 1,000 percent during this period. Nearly all taxes had to be paid in gold, while private citizens had to use debased coinage in commerce. The constituents of the Roman Empire, its soldiers and bureaucrats, were paid in gold.[22][23] Some parallels between 3rd century Roman Empire and present day are the increases in bureaucracy and government, multiple, expensive wars, rapidly rising government debt and abandonment of silver coinage in 1964. The literature of the Roman 3rd century constantly mentions impoverished citizens unable to pay their taxes, abandoning their residences and lands and disappearing.

The Sun Never Set on the British Empire

Lawrence James in his 1997 book, *The Rise and Fall of the British Empire*, wrote how in the 1800s, the sun never set on the British Empire. He described how the British Empire succumbed to the same overexpansion of military commitments, colonization and debt as Paul Kennedy explained in his book, *The Rise and Fall of the Great Powers.*[24]

Great Britain became the United Kingdom in 1801, but was already in the process of becoming a debtor nation for over 50 years before the 1800s. To transform a nation into an empire requires not only will and military power, but economic strength and money. The means to finance the country's wars, expansionary policies and provide its military with ships, weapons, munitions, soldiers and supplies likely emerged in 1717 when the first "Prime Minister" Sir Robert Walpole proposed a sinking fund to retire England's national debt. The General Fund Act embodying the sinking fund was enacted during the next Prime Minister Lord James Stanhope's tenure. Sinking fund monies were to be used to pay off the principal and interest of British public debt and for no other purpose. The funding was accomplished most often through the sale of government bonds. However, the monies were used in subsequent years to fund imperial wars, colonial expansion, costs of administering empire and peacetime expenses.[25] As long as interest was paid, the sinking fund need not pay off the principal if bonds that matured were replaced by the sale of new bonds. Under this regime, the sinking fund actually increased the United Kingdom's public debt over the decades.[26]

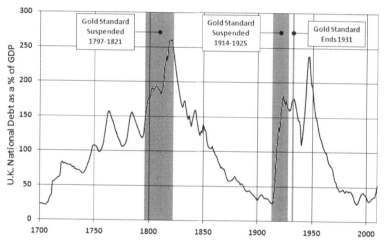

Figure 1-4: United Kingdom National Debt as a Percent of GDP, 1700 to 2010
Source: UK Public Spending,
http://www.ukpublicspending.co.uk/uk_debt[27]

Figure 1-4 shows how debt financed the British Empire. Percent of national debt over its gross domestic product illustrates how much larger national debt grew with respect to Britain's economic size. For instance, during the Napoleonic Wars from 1793 to 1815, national debt grew to 237% of GDP by 1816. Britain, at war with France for twenty years, had insufficient gold in its treasury, suspended the gold standard in 1797 and returned to it in 1821. Britain was engaged in at least 10 wars during the 1700s and 1800s, had to contend with many other skirmishes and incursions and maintained a military presence around the world. In the twentieth century, World War I and II costs helped propel the national debt per GDP ratio to 182% in 1923 and to 237% in 1947 respectively.[28]

How the United Kingdom's national debt affected price inflation is illustrated in Figure 1-5. During the wars with France from 1793 to 1815, war expenses became so great that the gold standard was suspended from 1797 to 1821. The resulting inflation peaked in 1800 at over 36%. Annual inflation rates fluctuated widely thereafter for 50 years until the United Kingdom made a concerted effort to reduce its debt levels through the next 60 years. The twentieth century ushered in World War I and II with its huge military costs. Annual inflation rates rose to 25% in 1917 and to 16.8% in 1940. Along with many other countries, the United Kingdom suspended the gold standard from 1914 to 1925 and then went completely off the gold standard in 1931.[29]

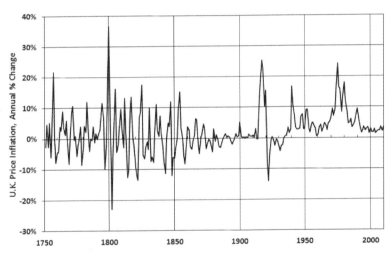

Figure 1-5: United Kingdom Price Inflation, Annual Percentage Change, 1751-2010
Source: United Kingdom Office for National Statistics[30]

America was untouched by World War II having been protected by two oceans. With its huge industrial-military base, technical abilities, sophisticated financial system and, most important of all, its creditor nation status, the United States became a superpower. The dollar established itself as the world's reserve currency. Bankrupted by two World Wars and prodded by internal and external anti-imperialistic and anti-colonial sentiments, the United Kingdom saw its power wane on the international stage. It held on to its colonies for a few years, but then intelligently gave them Commonwealth status and independence.[31]

Bridgewater Associates' founder, Ray Dalio, has written an interesting paper, "Why Countries Succeed and Fail Economically©." Dalio studied advanced countries and regions: United States, United Kingdom, Other Western Europe, Japan and Canada/Australia and emerging countries and regions: China, India, Other Asia, Latin America, Former USSR, Africa and Eastern Europe. His thesis concludes that a nation's share of the global economic pie increases and decreases due to long cycles not evident to anyone viewing economic events for short durations. Although his studies range back to 1500, Dalio concentrates on the years since 1820 and chronicles the successive countries and regions that have emerged as economic powers. He uses national income or gross domestic product (GDP) as a barometer of a countries'/regions' economic ascendancy and decline. Dalio cites many reasons propelling the latter cycles, but believes that debt is a major force behind these long-term cycles. Low but rising debt levels compared to GDP reinforce the economic ascendancy cycle phase. When debt becomes unsustainable, decline begins and accelerates. Dalio uses the British Empire as an example. Most notable from our viewpoint was a graph of the annual "Total Area of British Empire (% of World Land Mass)" whose rise and fall correlated with its real GDP per capita.[32]

PAPER MONEY IS ANCIENT

Johannes Gutenberg invented the first complete printing system or printing press in the early 15th century, but leaders in earlier times were using simpler printing presses or wood block printing processes. When it comes to inflating the money supply, a lack of sophisticated technology was no barrier.

Although there are clues to the use of paper money in China as long ago as 605, the first paper money in wide circulation has been traced back to 1165 during the Sung Dynasty of China. Bank notes were issued backed variously by copper coins and gold and silver ingots. The Yuan Dynasty, 1271–1368, also issued paper money but did not back it with gold or silver, making it arguably the first fiat currency. An undisciplined use of their printing presses caused inflation until the Yuan Dynasty's passing.[33]

Figure 1-6: German Housewife Using Papiermarks in Place of Firewood

Germany's Bank Law of 1875 required the Reichsbank to back one third or more of their issued notes with gold. The remainder had to be covered by "adequately guaranteed" 3-month discounted bills.[34] As the approaching storm clouds of World War I gathered over Europe, legislation passed in 1909 making the bank notes of Germany's Reichsbank and France's Banque de France into legal tender. Other countries followed. These bank notes were essentially government credit that would allow countries to finance the war with an invisible tax upon the citizens and without their consent. This legislation was one of the first instances, in the twentieth century, of the public accepting paper money as legal tender without full gold or silver backing. In 1914 as World War I commenced, the conversion of banknotes into gold was suspended. Now the stage was set for one of history's most famous hyperinflationary episodes. From 1914 until October 1923,

Germany printed physical banknotes at an extraordinary rate. A photo from that era shows a German housewife throwing bundles of banknotes into a furnace because it was cheaper than buying firewood. Finally the hyperinflation was stopped in 1924, when one Reichsmark was set equal to a trillion Papiermarks![35]

History teaches us that during times of great stress such as war, depression, economic turmoil or financial panic, countries resort to the issuance of devalued paper money and often to the suspension of paper money-to-gold convertibility. The precedent and the practice of using paper money without an adequate store of value backing it serves as a historical example to economists, bankers and politicians. Unfortunately they will also learn about its effectiveness in delaying the consequences of indebtedness.[36][37]

AMERICA'S CENTRAL BANK

America's central bank, the Federal Reserve Bank was established by the Federal Reserve Act of 1913. Its preamble stated, "An act to provide for the establishment of the Federal reserve banks, to furnish an elastic currency, to afford a means of rediscounting commercial paper, to establish a more effective supervision of banking in the United States, and for other purposes." The key to understanding is the phrase, "elastic currency." Congress and banking executives now had a method to supply money to member banks during financial crises and credit contractions. In their 1998 book, *The Great Depression: an international disaster of perverse economic policies*, Thomas E. Hall and J. David Ferguson wrote, "The Federal Reserve banks can create money and bank reserves! In 1914, their ability to expand bank reserves and the money supply was limited only by reserves the district banks themselves held." At that time, Congress called for the banks to have 40% gold backing for each dollar of bank reserves the Federal Reserve created.[38]

THE END OF OFFICAL DOLLAR GOLD CONVERTIBILITY

During the Great Depression, as thousands of U.S. banks began failing and fear prevailed, currency was being hoarded. Most countries were on the gold standard briefly from 1925 to 1931. As the depression spread worldwide, speculators as well as ordinary people began withdrawing gold from the banks whenever there was any hint that a country was discarding the gold standard and/or inflating its money supply. Great Britain, Japan and the Scandinavian countries were the first to abandon gold in 1931 due to huge outflows of capital and gold. As bank runs spread internationally and lending fell, more countries were forced off the gold standard.[39]

In February 1933 during the depths of the Great Depression, gold began flowing out of the U.S. banking system. To stem the tide, Executive Order 6102 in 1933 was carried out requiring American citizens to turn all gold bullion, gold certificates and all but $100 worth of gold coins over to the Federal Reserve. Rare and unusual gold coins were exempted. In total, U.S. citizens gave up 16 million ounces of gold. The Gold Reserve Act of 1934 was passed that changed the exchange rate from $20.67 to $35.00 per ounce of gold thus devaluing the paper dollar and reducing its purchasing power. The Act depreciated the dollar against all other currencies and improved the United States' ability to export. These actions stopped American citizens from redeeming paper money for gold and allowed the USA to pay its external debt with less gold.[40]

THE END OF THE BRETTON WOODS MONETARY SYSTEM AND GOLD BACKED MONEY

Due to global economic and trade problems including the Great Depression and countries' excessive debt during World War I, 45 countries met in Bretton Woods, New Hampshire and created the Bretton Woods Agreement in 1944 during World War II. The accord established a "gold exchange standard,"[41] which obligated member nations to fix their currency exchange rates with respect to the U.S. dollar and not have it vary up or down within one percent relative to the U.S. dollar. Other countries' currencies were not redeemable in gold, but other countries and central banks could exchange their dollars for gold. The United States implicitly agreed to convert dollars at $35 per ounce of gold. The Agreement established the International Monetary Fund, which would assist nations having economic difficulties and balance of payment problems with other nations.[42]

Upon first contemplation, the Bretton Woods Agreement appeared to stabilize the international monetary system except for one flaw.

The United States continued to "print" paper money or monetize debt and increase its trade deficits by inflating its money supply. Under a gentlemen's agreement, other countries did not trade their dollars in for gold, and instead, accrued dollar surpluses and inflated their currencies on top of the accumulated dollars. Essentially nearly everyone was inflating their money supplies. From 1944 to 1960, U.S. inflation as represented by the consumer price index, percent change average year-over-year fluctuated widely. Then from 1961 into the early 1980s, the inflation numbers climbed steadily. Since the inception of Bretton Woods, the United States started on an inexorable inflation path. Some of the main causes were the costly juxtaposition of the 1959-1975 Vietnam War and "Great Society" government programs that spent on items such as the war on poverty, Medicare, Medicaid, federal education funding and the National Endowment for the Arts and Humanities. A resulting balance of payments deficit caused the United States to begin losing its gold to other countries. Beginning in 1968, the free market price of gold started rising above $35 per ounce. Foreigners began draining gold from the U.S. Treasury. For instance, France began to exchange its dollar reserves for U.S. gold, which undermined America's international influence. Other countries also began to persist in exchanging their dollars for gold.[43] In 1968, the U.S. Congress passed the Gold Reserve Requirements Elimination Act, which eliminated the requirement to have gold back up 25% of U.S. currency.[44]

Under the Bretton Woods Agreement, the U.S. dollar had become the world's intervention and reserve currency thus preventing the United States from changing its foreign exchange rate. As the United States' balance of payments deficit continued to worsen and gold flowed out of the country, U.S. government authorities understood that the only way to devalue the dollar was to break its connection to the price of gold. In 1971 under extreme financial pressure, the federal government unilaterally closed America's dollar to gold window for foreign countries.[45] Nearly all countries quickly abandoned the gold standard and allowed their currencies to float against all other currencies. In fact, the last country to abandon gold backing for their currency was Switzerland. The Swiss Franc had 40% gold backing until 2000 when their new Federal Constitution abolished it.

Figure 1-7 shows the history of the dollar's march toward fiat money status.

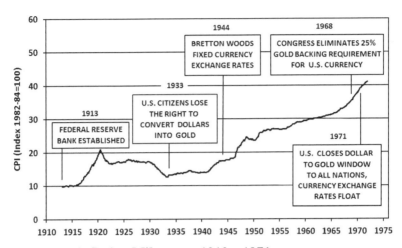

Figure 1-7: Inflation Milestones 1913 – 1971
Source: Federal Reserve Bank of St. Louis FRED® Economic Data

LESSONS LOST

The devaluation of the U.S. dollar amid the turmoil of World War I aftereffects and the Great Depression, the Bretton Woods monetary system flaws and the 1971 cessation of gold-backed money are familiar themes in history. Kings, warlords and heads of state devalued their coins by substituting cheaper metals for gold and silver. Coins became smaller and lighter or some ancient treasuries and mints milled the edges off existing coins. Our coins, once minted in gold and silver as legal tender, have given way to copper nickel sandwiches. Silver dimes and quarters were last minted in 1965. Ninety percent silver half dollars were last minted in 1964. Even our copper penny has become copper plated zinc since 1982. A copper penny weighs 3.11 grams. The zinc penny weighs only 2.5 grams.

Paper money or banknotes in the form of depositary receipts for grain, metals or nearly anything of worth have suffered the same printing press inflation as in modern times. Professors Carmen Reinhart and Kenneth Rogoff illustrate this observation in their book, *This Time Is Different: Eight Centuries of Financial Folly* ©. The authors have calculated and graphed the percent median inflation rate using a five year moving average for all countries from 1500 to 2007. We quote from their book:

"However spectacular some of the coinage debasements reported in tables 11.1 and 11.2, <u>without question the advent of the printing press elevated inflation to a whole new level.</u> Figure 12.1 illustrates the median inflation rate for all the countries in our sample from 1500 to 2007 (we used a five-year moving average to smooth out cycle and measurement errors). The figure shows a clear inflationary bias throughout history (although of course there are always periods of deflation due to business cycles, poor crops, and so on). <u>Starting in the twentieth century, however, inflation spiked radically.</u>"[46] [Underlining added]

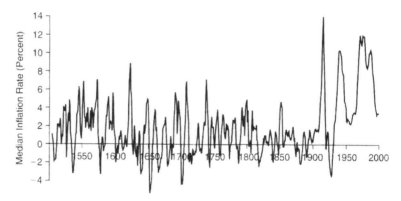

Figure 12.1. The median inflation rate: Five-year moving average for all countries, 1500–2007.

Figure 1-8: The median inflation rate: Five year moving average for all countries, 1500-2007, Figure 12.1 from *This Time is Different* ©
Source: Princeton University Press

This data presented by Professors Reinhart and Rogoff bolsters our argument that paper money with little or no physical store of value backing it will lead to a greater inflationary tendency. Johannes Gutenberg invented the movable-type printing press during the early 15th century greatly facilitating the technology of paper money printing and money supply manipulation. Figure 1-8 shows the strikingly larger spikes of median inflation that started occurring during the 20th century as modern nations began to either abandon gold backed money or forsake sound money principles.

The 20th century also witnessed nearly all of the great hyperinflationary episodes. Generation after generation forgets the lessons and the wisdom of sound money. Although Reinhart and Rogoff pointed out that there are periods of deflation, it's unlikely that with respect to inflation that anything will be different this time.

GOLD BACKED PAPER MONEY DOESN'T GUARANTEE SOUND MONEY DISCIPLINE

Although there are good arguments for gold-backed money such as those in Richard Duncan's 2009 book, *The Corruption of Capitalism,* the problem is that governments cannot adhere to the principles of sound money, and when their countries are under economic stress or armed conflict, will temporarily or permanently discard sound monetary principles or gold convertibility. The existence of multiple versions of gold standards, their proselytizers and their critics testifies to the complexity of creating a monetary system either on a national or international scale. We will examine a few of the weaknesses and strengths of two of the many historical gold standards.

The 100%-Reserve Gold Standard

Wikipedia describes a 100%-reserve gold standard, or full gold standard wherein all currency, coin and paper money, is 100% fully redeemable in gold. Detractors argue that the total amount of gold in the world is inadequate to fund global economic activity or that some new development might suddenly increase the gold supply leading to unwanted price volatility. Proponents believe that any quantity of gold can serve to back up representative money. They argue that as production of goods and services and the gold supply vary, prices would adjust, economic activity would eventually self-regulate and continue as usual, and gold backing would dampen inflationary tendencies.[47]

The Gold Exchange Standard

According to Wikipedia, the gold exchange standard lasted from about 1870 to 1914. Countries pegged their coins, either silver or another metal, to the gold standards of either the U.S. or the United Kingdom. The costs of World War I forced many participants to suspend gold convertibility during the war, which many considered a failure of the gold exchange standard. The next attempt to improve it led to another gold exchange standard created under the Bretton Woods Agreements following World War II. We chronicled in this chapter's previous section titled, "The End of the Bretton Woods Monetary System and Gold Backed Money," how the flaw of the U.S. and other countries being allowed to inflate their money supplies eventually led to the end of gold convertibility for all countries after 1971.

Who Guards the Gold Standard Guardians?

Economist Milton Friedman firmly believed that a fiat money supply was superior to a gold backed one and that it should grow at a constant 3% to 5% without a monetary authority monitoring and controlling it. Friedman, in a 1976 talk "Has Gold Lost Its Monetary Role?" opined, "If you could re-establish a world in which government's budget accounted for 10 percent of the national income, in which laissez-faire reigned, in which governments did not interfere with economic activities and in which full employment policies had been relegated to the dustbin, in such a world you might be able to restore a real gold standard. A real honest-to-God gold standard is not feasible because there is essentially no government in the world that is willing to surrender control over its domestic monetary policy."[48]

Austrian economist Ludwig von Mises (1881-1973), a gold standard advocate, nonetheless warned about any political bodies or governments that created and administered gold standards. In a collection of Ludwig von Mises' work, *The Causes of the Economic Crisis*, von Mises wrote, "However, it should certainly not be forgotten that under the "pure" gold standard governmental measures may also have a significant influence on the formation of the value of gold. In the first place, governmental actions determine whether to adopt the gold standard, abandon it, or return to it. …In this sense, all monetary standards may be "manipulated" under today's economic conditions. The advantage of the gold standard—whether "pure" or "gold exchange"—is due solely to the fact that, if once generally adopted in a definite form, and adhered to, it is no longer subject to specific political interferences."[49] In his book *The Theory of Money and Credit* there are similar opinions: "The safeguards erected by the liberal [classical] legislation of the nineteenth century to protect the bank-of-issue system against abuse by the State have proved inadequate. Nothing has been easier than to treat with contempt all the legislative provisions for the protection of the monetary standard. All governments, even the weakest and most incapable, have managed it without difficulty. Their banking policies have enabled them to bring about the state of affairs that the gold standard was designed to prevent: subjection of the value of money to the influence of political forces."[50]

In conclusion, history and economists such as Milton Friedman and Ludwig von Mises argue that governments can and will undermine sound monetary policies, whether gold-backed or not, that could have helped facilitate a stable environment for business and international trade. The balance of payments between countries would actually and eventually ... *balance* and its citizens could have faith in a stable currency. On the other hand, floating and sometimes volatile foreign exchange rates have likely caused many problems. For instance, instead of money going into productive endeavors such as manufacturing or capital expenditures, both of which require long-term planning horizons, money has been channeled into short-term speculative ventures where the risk is potentially lower. We have observed and are witnessing a large misallocation of scarce resources from productive endeavors into speculative ones.

THE LONG ROAD TO FINANCIAL CRISIS

The demise of the U.S. gold standard, transformed the dollar into fiat money, which is not convertible into anything else, can be "printed" into existence and requires a government fiat, decree or order that their fiat money be used as legal tender, which according to Wikipedia, is a "medium of payment allowed by law or recognized by a legal system to be valid for meeting a financial obligation."[51] Every precondition was in place for all governments of all nations to control the size of their money supplies, to monetize their debt and, within the restrictions imposed only by market and political forces, to fiscally stimulate their economies.

Many observers believe that when a nation turns its money into fiat money, it is headed for trouble. Nobel-prize winner, Milton Friedman, in his book, *Money Mischief*, wrote, "These developments are not unique to the United States or to recent decades. Since time immemorial, sovereigns—whether kings, emperors, or parliaments—were tempted to resort to increasing the quantity of money as a means of acquiring resources to wage wars, to construct monuments, or for other purposes. They have often succumbed to the temptation. Whenever they have, inflation has followed close behind." He advised that the task of slowing inflation always entails job losses and a temporary decrease in economic growth rates. Friedman warned that delaying the task of tamping down high inflation will incur greater costs later.[52]

Economist Ludwig von Mises (1881-1973), believed in "a policy of unrestricted laissez-faire, of free markets and the unhampered exercise of the right of private property, with government strictly limited to the defense of person and property within its territorial area."[53] Mises opined at a University of Chicago Law School conference that "We have not to choose between financing the increased government expenditure by collecting taxes and borrowing from the public, on the one hand, and financing it by inflation, on the other hand. Inflation can never be an instrument of a fiscal policy continued over a long period of time. Continued inflation inevitably leads to catastrophe."[54]

In following chapters, we will chronicle how the near universal adoption of irredeemable fiat money continued to create long term inflation and credit expansion leading finally to unsustainable debt, which in turn led to the credit squeeze, the Great Recession, deleveraging, disinflation and a long, slow economic recovery.

CHAPTER TWO

How Monetary and Fiscal Policies of Governments Affect You

"The Inflation Chickens Come Home to Roost"

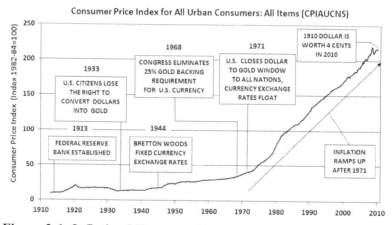

Figure 2-1: Inflation Milestones 1910 - 2010
Source: Federal Reserve Bank of St. Louis FRED® Economic Data

INTRODUCTION

Chapter One explained how a combination of economic stress, the costs of armed conflict and government decisions caused all nations to abandon sound and/or gold-backed monetary systems and inflate their money supplies. Besides the dollar, all nations' currencies have become fiat paper money that cannot be exchanged for gold.

Figure 2-1 clearly shows how inflation ramped up after 1971, which is the equivalent of an average 4.6% increase in prices year after year. The rise in prices in any one year usually appears rather benign, but the compounding effect of a small percentage rise year after year for 40 years beginning in 1970 is not. In 1970, a pound loaf of bread cost 25 cents and a gallon of gas 36 cents. In 2010, they cost $3.92 and $2.98 respectively.[55]

In more recent years, the public has complained that inflation feels greater than the federal government's consumer price index figures. In Figure 2-2, we've separated out the costs of food, gasoline, medical care and tuition, other school fees, and childcare and compared them to the All Items CPI for all urban consumers. Pundits theorize that the largest inflationary increases in two categories: Tuition, other school fees, and childcare and Medical Care are due to Federal and state government financial programs. The federal government has allowed students to take out larger loans than previously, but hasn't permitted them to renege on their college loans in bankruptcy. In response, colleges raised their tuition and related costs as students' college loan levels rose. For instance, the U.S. Department of Labor stated that institutions of higher learning increased their managerial and administrative employees at a rate 50% greater than they hired instructors from 2001 to 2011.[56]

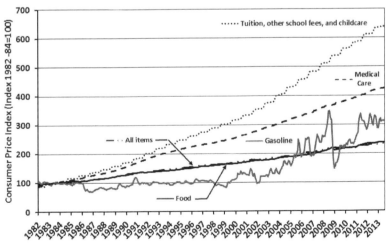

Figure 2-2: Consumer Price Index for All Urban Consumers: All Items and Other Selected Categories 1982 - 2013
Source: Federal Reserve Bank of St. Louis FRED® Economic Data

The National Center for Policy Analysis believes that medical care costs increase when third parties (employers, insurance companies or government) pay rather than the patient. They estimate that patients pay only 12 cents for every $1 of medical services in the U.S. health care system as a whole. When patients pay out of their own pocket, they are much more careful. When Medicare and Medicaid were instituted in 1965, medical costs didn't exceed 6% of GDP. In 2010 it was 17%.[57]

Gasoline is another highly visible, weekly reminder of the cost of living for the consumer. Causes for gasoline price inflation are peak oil, government tax increases that comprise about 14% of gasoline's price, increased demand especially from countries such as India and China. By 2020, China plans to build 42,000 miles of interprovincial highways and India 12,000 miles. In contrast, there are 86,000 miles of U.S. interstate highways.[58]

Surprisingly food inflation rate has closely tracked the CPI's All Items inflation rate. However, consumers feel differently. In this category, we suspect that the Bureau of Labor Statistics' (BLS) changed calculation methodology is the cause. In the past, the inflation rate was calculated by using a fixed-basket of goods and services with the same components and same weighting for month after month. Now the BLS substitutes inflation components such as hamburger for steak under a concept called "hedonic quality modeling." We all know how expensive steak has become.[59]

Although controversial, economics consultant John Williams runs the Shadow Government Statistics web site. Williams claims that the Consumer Price Index has been calculated differently since the early 1980s. The result, according to Williams, has been to understate the true amount of inflation in the economy.

Williams stated in one of his web site's articles, "No. 438—PUBLIC COMMENT ON INFLATION MEASUREMENT," dated May 15, 2012, "While the CPI at one time was the measure desired by the public, government efforts turned the CPI away from measuring the price changes in a fixed-weight basket of goods and services to a quasi-substitution-based basket of goods, which destroyed the concept of the CPI as a measure of the cost of living of maintaining a constant standard of living.

The use of hedonic quality modeling in adjusting the prices of goods and services has destroyed the concept of the CPI as a measure of out-of-pocket expenses."

For example, according to Williams, the Cumulative Annual Inflation Shortfall from 2006 to 2011 has been minus 5.1%.[60]

As we live through our latest financial crises and Great Recession aftermath, reading about its decades-spanning causes will form the basis for understanding what confronts us.

BUDGET DEFICITS HAVE CREATED INFLATION AND RECORD GOVERNMENT DEBT

The United States, because it has run budget deficits for decades, has had to make up the shortfall in tax revenues by selling U.S. Treasury bonds. As this debt was monetized, U.S. money supply expanded over and above that called for by increases in population, productivity and technological change. The combination of money supply growth plus private sector credit creation generated a demand greater than normal for the production of goods and services and often resulted in price and wage inflation. Many argue for economic intervention for the purpose of cyclically counteracting recessions and for promoting manageable inflation to enhance prosperity. Those arguing against intervention believe it adds unnecessarily to price and wage inflation and eventually intensifies boom and bust cycles.

Stanford University economist John Taylor disapproves of federal government "discretionary countercyclical actions and interventions to prevent or mitigate recessions or to speed up recoveries." In his July 19, 2011 blog, "What Does Anti-Keynesian Mean?," Taylor writes, "Indeed, the models that I have built support the use of policy rules, such as the Taylor rule for monetary policy or the automatic stabilizers for fiscal policy, which are the polar opposite of Keynesian discretion. As a practical prescription for improving the economy, the empirical evidence is clear in my view that discretionary Keynesian policy does not work and the experience of the past three years confirms this view." He advocates monetary policy such as his Taylor rule for setting short term Fed funds rate and automatic stabilizers for fiscal policy.[61] The following is economist John Taylor's example of government's financial stimulus policy, how deeply government can deficit spend thus adding to the total debt and the unintended consequences of such actions.

John Taylor and coauthor John Cogan, in a January 2011 Hoover Institution commentary, "Where Did the Stimulus Go?" state that three years after the Federal government's $1 trillion deficit spending, there is still high unemployment and low economic growth. The authors' first graph clearly shows the spikes in personal disposable income due to the 2008 and 2009 financial stimuli. However, the disposable consumption expenditure changes were hardly noticeable. Consumers either saved the stimulus money or used it to pay off debt. The authors cite the Friedman-Modigliani theory, "The permanent income," in which people don't increase their consumption because of temporary increases in transfer payments or momentary tax rebates. Direct Federal government purchases added up to only $20 billion of which $4 billion was for infrastructure projects. Since the 1970s, Federal laws and regulation have slowed all such "shovel ready" projects. In their graph 2, they show how $170 billion of Federal grants to state and local government were used to reduce debt rather than increase purchases. The Federal government sent borrowed funds to consumers and to states and local governments, but they spent negligible dollars for purchases of goods and services. Taylor and Cogan conclude, "In effect, the increased net borrowing at the federal level was matched by reduced net borrowing by households and state and local government. ...So there was little if any net stimulus. The irony is that basic economic theory and practical experience predicted this would happen."[62] Taylor and Cogan are against "temporary, targeted and timely" Keynesian stimuli and for those that are "permanent, pervasive and predictable." Taylor believes that one stimulus meeting the latter criteria are permanent tax cuts.[63]

Eventually state, local and federal government debt may overwhelm us, cause greater declines in GDP, and diminish its citizens' net worth. In their book, *This Time is Different: Eight Centuries of Financial Folly*, Professors Kenneth Rogoff and Carmen Reinhart write that three years after a financial banking crisis similar to the one we had in late 2008, public debt typically rose 86% and in some cases rose 300%.[64] In an August 2010 paper, "Growth in a Time of Debt," the authors found that when a country's debt to GDP ratio rises above 90%, which America's has, its "median growth rates fall by 1%, and average growth falls considerably more."[65] In the long run, the markets and general social trends will decide how this one hundred year experiment in government intervention, inflation and debt will end.

The TreasuryDirect web site computes our national "debt to the penny," at: http://www.treasurydirect.gov/NP/BPDLogin? application=np. As of 2012, it's over $16.2 trillion. You can watch this debt figure roll over on the Debt Clock at Avenue of Americas, New York City. At one point when the debt reached $10 trillion, the clock ran out of digits. A new clock is planned that will read up to a quadrillion dollars, that is 1 followed by 15 zeros. Let's see what the progression is, a million, a billion, a trillion and a quadrillion (1,000,000,000,000,000).

GOVERNMENT IGNORES MILTON FRIEDMAN'S MONETARIST THEORIES

Milton Friedman, Nobel Prize winning economist, formulated the k-percent rule, which would increase the money supply by a fixed amount perhaps two to four percent every year, year after year. The calculation for money supply increases would include:[66]

1. the nation's population growth and;
2. U.S. labor productivity advances.

In a 2006 Library of Economics and Liberty interview, Friedman voiced the opinion that a computer could be programmed to increase the money supply by 4% a year making the Federal Reserve redundant.[67] However, the Federal government seldom followed Friedman's k-percent rule. In reality, the government inflated the money supply beyond Friedman's theoretical limit, which contributed to decades of price inflation.[68]

Figures 2-3 and 2-4 show how M2 Seasonally Adjusted Money Supply accelerated from 1970 onward far above Friedman's k-percent rule of two to four percent. The equivalent year-over-year percent change translates to 6.8% every year for forty years, which the reader can compare to the linear trendline in Figure 2-4.

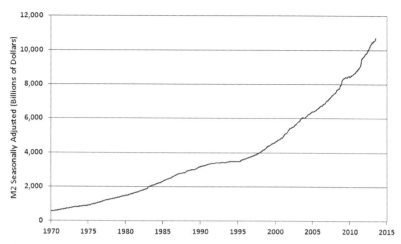

Figure 2-3: M2SL Money Supply Seasonally Adjusted 1970 - 2013
Source: Federal Reserve Bank of St. Louis

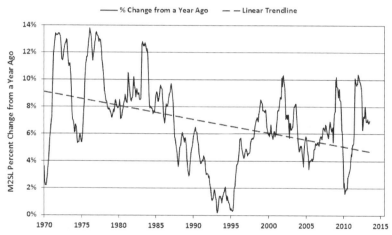

Figure 2-4: M2SL Money Supply Seasonally Adjusted Percent Change from Year Ago
Source: Federal Reserve Bank of St. Louis

A comparison, illustrated in Figure 2-5 between U.S. Consumer Price Index (CPI) and U.S. population growth from 1971 to 2010 shows the disparity caused by excessive money supply growth. The latter has caused greater increases in CPI or price inflation than if Friedman's k-percent rule were followed. The average annualized or year-over-year percent change in the Consumer Price Index is notably higher than the estimated 1.04% U.S. population growth year over year since 1970. When allowed for forty years, the result is inflation as graphically shown in Figure 2-1.

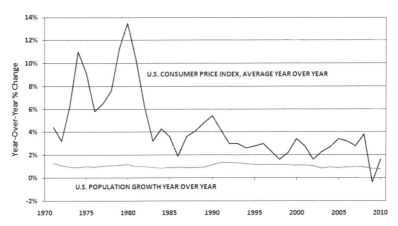

Figure 2-5: U.S. Consumer Price Index versus Population Growth, Year-Over-Year Percent Change
Source: St. Louis Federal Reserve Bank, U.S. Bureau of the Census

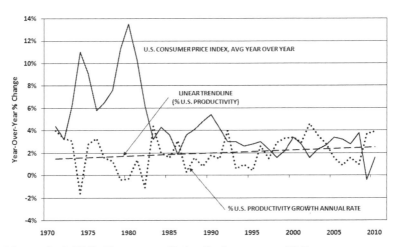

Figure 2-6: U.S. Consumer Price Index versus U.S. Productivity Growth, Year-Over-Year Percent Change
Source: St. Louis Federal Reserve Bank, U.S. Bureau of Labor Statistics

In Figure 2-6, average annualized or year-over-year percent change in U.S. productivity growth is approximately 2.02% from 1970 to 2010. These graphs show the disparity between price inflation and the combined effects of percent changes in population and productivity growth. In Chapter One, subheading *"The Effect of Credit on Inflation,"* we stated, "In 1968, the United States Total Credit Market Debt was $1.37 trillion. In 2011, it reached $54.1 trillion or an increase of 40X." The average annual credit growth rate year over year for those last 40 years was 8.92%, which was another source of inflation. The comparisons are summarized in Table 2-1.

Table 2-1: Average Year over Year Percent Change for 40 Years

Comparing M2SL Money Supply, Total Credit Market Debt Growth & Inflation Rate with Population & Productivity Growth	Average Year over Year Percent Change for 40 years
U.S. M2SL Money Supply Growth	6.80%
U.S. Total Credit Market Debt Growth*	8.92%
U.S. Inflation Rate	4.60%
U.S. Population Growth	1.04%
U.S. Productivity Growth	2.02%

* Refer to Figure 1-2: Total Credit Market Debt, M2 Money Supply

Friedman's economic theories are arguably among the finest. However, governments and politicians ignored his theories. Libertarian economist Murray Rothbard, known for his book, *America's Great Depression*, thought that Friedman's idea of allowing the State to centrally direct monetary policy and to expand and contract the money supply was automatically inflationary. In an article titled "Milton Friedman Unraveled," Rothbard opined, "Friedman's advice to restrict this power to an [money supply] expansion of 3–4% per year ignores the crucial fact that any group, coming into the possession of the absolute power to 'print money,' will tend to . . . print it!"[69]

In a July 1985 speech titled, "Economists and Economic Policy," Friedman expressed doubts about the government's ability to follow his k-percent rule for adjusting the money supply. "The Federal Reserve System puts a great deal of power in the hands of a few people and it is so constructed that it has been in their self-interest to pursue a policy which, I believe, has been very harmful for the public rather than helpful.... Clearly, it was not in the self-interest of the Federal Reserve hierarchy to follow the hypothetical policy [of a monetary rule]. It was therefore a waste of time to try to persuade them to do so."[70]

So far, we have shown how the government increased the money supply to a greater extent than was necessary according to Friedman's k-percent rule. However, in the previous chapter, we defined inflation as an increase in the supply of money and credit and we must include the growth of credit as a major cause of inflation. For the last forty years, U.S. consumer credit expanded at an equivalent year-over-year percent change of 7.4% every year in contrast to 6.8% for money supply increases. Figure 2-7 shows the similarity in the increase between U.S. consumer credit and the increase in money supply inflation as shown in Figure 2-3.

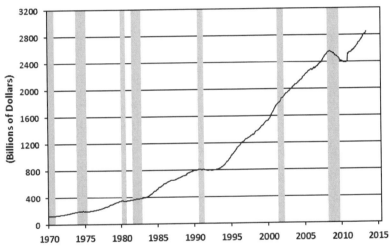

Figure 2-7: Total U.S. Consumer Credit Outstanding, Grey areas denote recessions
Source: Board of Governors of the Federal Reserve System
Note: Gray areas are recessions according to the National Bureau of Economic Research

DOES INCREASING GOVERNMENT DEBT EVENTUALLY DECREASE GDP?

Whenever politicians or central banks implement fiscal stimuli to help recover from a recession and when the government is running budget deficits, government bonds must be sold to borrow the funds if tax revenues don't cover the shortfall. The former call upon the work of many experts who use theories and models that show every dollar of fiscal stimuli or tax cuts or increases will multiply its effects in the economy. The multiplier, depending upon which theoretician called upon, can range from negative to positive.

Spending Multipliers

In their 2009 paper, "New Keynesian versus Old Keynesian Government Spending Multipliers," economist John Taylor and others decided to use new Keynesian models to simulate the macro-economy when subjected to spending multipliers. They compared their results to simulations using older Keynesian models. They found that multipliers due to permanent government purchases were smaller when analyzed using new Keynesian than in old Keynesian models. This effect was more pronounced in the recent 2009 U.S. stimulus packages. Their results showed multipliers less than one. They hypothesized that government spending usurped personal consumption and private investment. In time, as government spending lessens, the multipliers became negative.[71]

In their "Quarterly Review and Outlook First Quarter 2010," Van R. Hoisington and Lacy H. Hunt, Ph.D. of Hoisington Investment Management Company present viewpoints about our government's fiscal stimulus policies financed by borrowed money. "The federal government cannot create prosperity by spending funds that it does not have. It can, however, spend us into poverty by taking dollar balances from highly productive individuals and their business entities, through borrowing or taxing. This process of transferring these assets from income and wealth generators to other government applications has profound economic consequences."

Hoisington and Hunt cite several individuals' studies that support their viewpoint. Foremost in their review is Harvard economist Robert Barro. He wrote in a Wall Street Journal January 22, 2009 article, "Government Spending Is No Free Lunch," that "team Obama" apparently believes that government spending multiplies economic output by about 1.5 to 1. In the article, Barro stated, "A much more plausible starting point is a multiplier of zero. In this case, the GDP (gross domestic product) is given, and a rise in government purchases requires an equal fall in the total of other parts of GDP -- consumption, investment and net exports."[72]

Tax Multipliers

The federal government has fed massive fiscal stimuli into the economy in the last three years. The trillion dollar deficits predicted in the future indicate that large tax rate increases may be approaching. The Obama administration estimates that tax revenues could increase by $700 billion for the decade. There are a plethora of other taxes and tax increases that are being contemplated and few spending decreases of any importance.

To find a historical precedent for higher taxes after a financial crisis, one need only study the Great Depression and its aftermath. During the 1930s, President Roosevelt argued that "we should plan to have a definitely balanced budget...and seek a continuing reduction of the national debt," and instituted an extraordinarily large number of taxes to carry out that goal. Up to 1931, the marginal tax rate for top income bracket individuals was 25%. Then from 1932 to 1935, that rate was elevated to 63% and then from 1936 to 1939, it was 79% and 81.1% in 1940.[73]

Upon further study in late 2009, Barro and Charles Redlick concluded that the government defense spending multiplier was about 0.6 to 0.8 and that the non-defense spending multiplier was unlikely to be larger. They also found evidence that tax cuts increased total economic output, "with a one percentage point decrease in the average marginal tax rate leading to an increase of about 0.6% in the growth rate of real per capita GDP."[74]

In a November 2008 Wall Street Journal article, "Why Permanent Tax Cuts Are the Best Stimulus," Stanford economist John Taylor wrote that existing tax rates should remain permanent so that business would not fear tax increases on income, capital gains and dividends. He believes that tax cuts should be "permanent, pervasive and predictable."[75]

These experts' research suggests that tax increases will lower GDP and tax revenues and, in the long run, any GDP increases are temporary in nature.

THE PROBLEM WITH MONETARY SYSTEMS

You may have concluded that we believe in gold-backed paper money, but it has its drawbacks. The biggest one is that leaders and governments, whether we look at examples from history or from current events, will skirt the discipline of "sound money" and devalue their currency with respect to gold or they may abandon gold altogether as the United States did in 1971. Another problem is that the amount of gold backing a paper currency or a fiat currency must keep up with population and productivity growth. Some have suggested using a computerized formula that adjusts gold or money supply dependent upon population and productivity. However, what happens if a country's demography changes. For instance, the population might become very young or might age, as Japan's has. What are the effects? Can a computer do the same for productivity? Is it really that easy? The formula to calculate the values of both variables can be very complicated and make the chances for mistakes very high. A gold standard, under normal circumstances, restrains nations running trade imbalances and imposes lower prices and wages upon its citizen. The correction entails probable deflation and job losses that a country may not wish to suffer through. However, since every economic process, such as multi-year trade imbalances, will eventually revert back to the mean, delaying reforms will mean greater suffering later.

During the period 1460 to 1530, European silver mining production grew 5X, which stimulated inflation before Spain had, during the 1500s and 1600s, bringing home shiploads of gold and silver from the New World. Although these precious metals transformed Spain into a wealthy nation, its citizens traded it for goods mostly from other European nations. An overabundance of gold and silver in Europe caused a 300% to 400% price inflation called the "Price Revolution." Throughout this period, Spain failed to develop their own industry that could have manufactured goods internally and offset a scarcer supply of foreign goods. To summarize, too much gold and silver money chased after a too small supply of merchandise.[76] In the present time, since gold is increasingly harder to find and mine, the reverse could happen wherein enough gold couldn't be injected into growing economies, thus causing deflation.

So why do the boom and bust cycles continue? Why haven't they designed the perfect international monetary system that will stop inflation or deflation, zero out countries' balance of trade deficits and surpluses, and steadily create ever greater prosperity?

Part of the problem is that people design and implement national monetary systems. For instance, economist Murray Rothbard argued that Friedmanites, the followers of Milton Friedman's monetarist theories, once they gained the power to manipulate the money supply, would almost always choose expansion. Friedman's monetarist rules work in theory, but countries are often forced to circumvent them especially during crises and wars.

Sound money policies would help create a stable environment for businesses especially those engaged in international trade. Floating foreign exchange rates have likely caused many economic problems. For instance, instead of money going into productive endeavors such as manufacturing or capital expenditures, both of which require long-term planning horizons, money has been channeled into short-term speculative ventures where the risk is potentially lower. We have and are witnessing a large misallocation of scarce resources from productive endeavors into speculative ones.

Milton Friedman was a champion of the floating exchange rate system, which arose spontaneously and without any countries' intention or design after the United States abandoned gold-dollar convertibility in 1971. Under this system, a huge foreign exchange market resolves the exchange rate of a nation's currency with respect to other currencies through the interaction of market demand and supply forces.[77] Any country that incurs a balance of payments deficit is importing more goods than they are exporting. That country's currency weakens since its importers sell it to pay exporters in foreign countries. In the foreign exchange rate market, this drives their country's currency down with respect to other currencies thus making their exports less expensive and its imports more expensive.[78] More of their exports are sold abroad and fewer imports are bought in their country. In this manner, the balance of trade deficit is reduced until equilibrium is reached.[79]

The fly in the ointment is countries circumventing the floating exchange rate system by pegging their currencies to the dollar or manipulating their money supply. Milton Friedman described the People's Republic of China pegging or fixing the exchange rate of the Chinese yuan relative to the U.S. dollar so that their imports are cheaper in other countries. Because the United States has been maintaining a current accounts deficit and China a surplus for years, billions of our dollars have traveled to China. If China allowed the free conversion of dollars into yuan, then excessive amounts of yuan would produce price inflation in China. China has used the excess dollars to buy hundreds of billions of dollars of U.S. Treasury securities to prevent in-country inflation.[80][81] Because the dollar acts as a reserve currency for all other countries, the United States has borrowed other countries' savings and run a balance of trade deficit for decades, which helped propel the U.S. into debtor nation status.

The nature of national monetary systems and the floating foreign exchange rate system has allowed nations to engage in currency wars that are disguised trade wars. During the Great Recession, the Federal Reserve embarked on a program of Quantitative Easing 1 (QE1) to increase United States money supply generally by using open market purchases of U.S. debt which eventually totaled $1.7 trillion. Such actions have the effect of devaluing the dollar relative to other countries' currencies thereby making our exports cheaper, lending rates lower and hopefully helping reduce or slow our balance of payments deficit. The Federal Reserve's Quantitative Easing 2 (QE2) program ran from November 2010 until end of the second quarter of 2011. The bond purchases totaled $600 billion over eight months.[82] The Federal Reserve under Chairman Bernanke declared the start of Quantitative Easing 3 or QE3 on September 13, 2012, which consists of an open-ended $40 billion per month purchasing schedule of agency mortgage-backed securities. The goals of this program and the maintenance of a very low interest rate environment are to stimulate the economy and lower interest rates further.[83] Of course other countries understand that all of this quantitative easing is the equivalent of a U.S. devaluation of the dollar and know it will make their exports more expensive. To counter the Federal Reserve Bank's actions, other countries are trying to manipulate foreign exchange rates in their favor by imposing capital controls on the flow of money into their countries, levying tariffs and buying or selling currencies in the foreign exchange markets.[84]

Currency Wars

James Rickards, investment banker and risk manager, warns us that this continuing currency war just described is heating up and will lead to a crisis worse than the 2008 financial meltdown. In his book, *Currency Wars: The Making of the Next Global Crisis*, Rickards reviews two historical currency wars: Currency War I from 1921 to 1936 involving the abandonment and reintroduction of gold backed money and Currency War II from 1967 to 1987 leading to the international termination of gold to dollar convertibility. Currency War III, which began in 2010, is still being waged. Rickards explains how these currency wars escalated from robbing economic growth and trade from each other, to reprisal and to armed conflict. Rickards details how Currency War III is being fought on an immense scale, how faith in the dollar could be destroyed and how the national security of the United States and the stability of the global financial system are at stake. Rickards cautions, "Today the risk is the collapse of the monetary system itself—a loss of confidence on paper currencies and a massive flight to hard assets. Given these risks of catastrophic failure, Currency War III may be the last currency war—or, to paraphrase Woodrow Wilson, the war to end all currency wars."[85]

Our contention is that economic models and national monetary systems are imperfect in the real world. No matter that a gold standard backs the currency or that a fixed or floating currency exchange rate system is supposed to zero out countries' balance of payments. Human nature and Taleb's black swans, which are unpredictable and extremely rare financial crises, will undermine economic models and national monetary systems and lead to the next economic decline. Economist Nouriel Roubini believes we haven't learned our lessons about high debt levels and that, "Deficits in excess of 10% of GDP can be found in many advanced economies, including America's, and debt-to-GDP ratios are expected to rise sharply – in some cases doubling in the next few years."[86] He opines that government policy "is now creating a new global asset bubble that will cause a bigger financial crisis in the next few years."[87] Although most observers are often surprised by financial crises and pronounce them black swans, Roubini, in his book, *Crisis Economics*, argued that, "Contrary to conventional wisdom, crises are not black swans but white swans: the elements of boom and bust are remarkably predictable. Look into the recent past, and you can find dozens of financial crises. Further back in time, before the Great Depression, many more lurk in the historical record. Some of them hit single nations; others reverberated across countries and continents, wreaking havoc on a global scale. Yet most are forgotten today, dismissed as relics of a less enlightened era."[88] Thus anyone perusing the history of such crises and government's responses to them will conclude that when the next economic crisis arrives, governments will likely sidestep sound monetary principles.

In summary, countries have circumvented their national monetary systems whether backed by gold or not or whether constrained under the Bretton Woods' fixed exchange rate system. They have thwarted the floating exchange rate system by using pegged currencies, trade tariffs and capital flow restrictions.

GLOBAL MONETARY SYSTEM REFORMS

Nations and multilateral institutions will get serious about the design and implementation of a better international monetary system when another global financial crisis arrives. The crisis will highlight the faults of national monetary systems, whose imperfections authorities will attempt to avoid by improving the international monetary system and instituting a global currency in place of the current reserve currencies.

The United Nations Conference on Trade and Development (UNCTAD) called for a global currency to replace the dollar as the world's reserve currency in their "Trade and Development Report 2009." UNCTAD reported that the existing international monetary system's inadequacies are a major cause of global economic crises. For many decades, the present floating exchange rate and international monetary system has allowed countries such as the United States to run a current-account deficit as long as other countries would lend to it or for China to run a current-account surplus by pegging its currency to the dollar to help keep its exports cheaper than other countries. The report states that the resulting current account disequilibria are ultimately unsustainable. Under a United Nations' inspired global monetary system, countries would manage their foreign exchange rates to keep them stable and to control inflation. Destabilizing cross country capital flows would be supervised. International liquidity would be provided where required. As nations withdraw from the dollar as a reserve currency, a major dollar crisis could be mitigated by having their central banks deposit dollar reserves in the International Monetary Fund's "special account" that would be denominated in the IMF's SDRs (special drawing rights). SDRs are presently valued as a weighted average of the major currencies. The IMF would change the properties of SDRs to serve as a global currency that could be used to make international payments. The United Nations report suggests that an institution such as the International Monetary Fund administer such a global monetary system.[89]

A 2010 International Monetary Fund paper, "Reserve Accumulation and International Monetary Stability," reviews ideas for improving the international monetary system (IMS), to make it more resilient and prevent "repeated and costly international financial crises." The paper cites as destabilizing factors: unequal balances of trade leading to current account deficits and surpluses among nations and large movements of capital between countries. These phenomena lead to asset bubbles and busts, countries building large reserves and concentrations of the latter in a few reserve currencies such as the dollar or Euro. To help counteract these occurrences, a reformed international monetary system could provide a global currency, which the IMF suggests in their paper could be called the bancor. The original bancor was first conceived by economist John Maynard Keynes after World War II. During the Bretton Woods conference, the United States prevented its implementation in favor of the dollar as a reserve currency. The new bancor could be used by all countries in a similar manner to the Euro currency. This is an unlikely outcome since many countries may resist its use. More likely to be adopted is a system of national currencies that would be used in parallel with, and tied to, the bancor. The paper reviews several reasons for implementing a global currency and international monetary system.[90] In their companion paper, "Reserve Accumulation and International Monetary Stability: Supplementary Information," the Strategy, Policy and Review Department presents more information about the administration and operation of the bancor. For instance, a global central bank would issue bancors, conduct policy issues and act as lender of last resort when nations run into liquidity problems. The bancor itself would be defined in terms of an international basket of goods and services.[91]

Proposals calling for a global currency even partially backed by gold are rare. Under any global currency system and to a greater extent under a gold-backed global currency system, nations would relinquish a great deal of control over their money supply and monetary policy. In spite of this, World Bank President Robert Zoellick, in a 2010 Financial Times opinion piece, called for a "cooperative monetary system" whose design would have to include the dollar, the euro, the yen, the pound and the renminbi; and "should also consider employing gold as an international reference point of market expectations about inflation, deflation and future currency values." The media mistakenly reported that Zoellick was calling for a return to the gold standard. Zoellick was later quoted as saying that a return to the gold standard wasn't practical. The fact that his remarks were dismissed or ignored by mainstream economists and officials is a good indicator of the level of anti-gold standard sentiment.[92]

We cannot predict what form national and global monetary systems will take, but suspect that they will not include a gold standard.

WHY HAVE BOOM AND BUST CYCLES GOTTEN WORSE?

A myriad of pundits believe that government intervention rather than smoothing out boom and bust cycles actually increases their amplitude. They argue that whenever government attempts to stimulate a slowing economy, it has created false, liquidity-driven booms followed by bigger busts. The recent examples are the technology stock market boom of the late 1990s and 2000-2003 bust and then the residential real estate boom leading up to the crash commencing in the late 2000s. Below we describe some causes for the greater amplitudes of boom and bust cycles.

John Taylor, Stanford University Economics professor, theorizes that at least partial blame for our latest financial crisis must be placed on the doorstep of the federal government. In his 2009 book, *Getting Off Track: How Government Actions and Interventions Caused, Prolonged, and Worsened the Financial Crisis*, Professor Taylor, in 1992, formulated the Taylor Rule to guide policy makers in setting the short term Federal Funds rate. Taylor described the Taylor rule as follows: "To be precise, the Taylor rule says that the interest rate should be one-and-a-half times the inflation rate plus one-half times the GDP gap plus one. (The GDP gap measures how far GDP is from its normal trend level.)"[93]

Taylor cites an October 18, 2011 chart from The Economist magazine that was based on his paper presented at the August 2007 Jackson Hole conference. The chart shows how Federal Reserve Chairman Alan Greenspan lowered the Federal funds rate from 6.5% to 1.0% from mid-2000 to early 2004. From that point Greenspan raised the rate to 5.25% in 2006. Taylor shows that the Taylor rule dictates a straight line rise in the Fed funds rate from 1.73% in January 2002 to 5.25% in June 2005. Thus the Taylor rule, if followed, would have kept rates much higher than Greenspan's actions.[94] Taylor opposed Greenspan's deviation from the Taylor rule, the "too loose" monetary policy that Taylor had contended led to the housing boom and bust. He used an empirical counterfactual argument, which economists use to study cause and effect, to show that there would have been no boom and no bust if Greenspan had adhered to the Taylor rule. His results indicate that from 2003 to 2006 counterfactual housing starts would have grown over 18%, but that actual housing starts from 2000 to 2006 were about 55%.[95][96] In his book's Epilogue, Taylor concludes, "They caused it [the financial crisis] by deviating from historical precedents and principles for setting interest rates that had worked well for twenty years. They prolonged it by misdiagnosing the problems in the bank credit markets and thereby responding inappropriately, focusing on liquidity rather than risk. They made it worse by supporting certain financial institutions and their creditors, but not others in an ad hoc way, without a clear and understandable framework."[97]

The primary contributor to price and asset inflation has been the creation of vast amounts of credit that fueled the booms. The government wasn't alone in jacking up money supply and liquidity through low fractional reserve banking requirements, low government interest rates and fiscal stimuli. Another major contributor to increased credit during the recent boom has been the appropriately named "shadow banking system" consisting of financial entities such as hedge funds, structured investment vehicles (SIV), conduits, money market funds, monolines, investment banks, and other non-bank financial institutions outside the normal banking system. For explanations of all these entities, we refer you to Wikipedia, the online free encyclopedia, where you can enter the phrase, "shadow banking system." According to U.S. Treasury Secretary Timothy Geithner, their total assets in early 2007 were twice as large as those of entire traditional banking system in the United States, whose assets totaled $10 trillion.[98]

One of the shadow banks' favorite tactics was to borrow money at low short term rates and lend it out at longer maturity rates that were substantially higher. Since they were not commercial banks, the shadow banks operated outside the regulatory system that required sufficient capital reserves needed during fiscal emergencies or if depositors made "bank runs." Thus their ratio of debt (how much they could lend out) to capital reserves was extremely high. These non-banks leveraged money by as much as 30 to 60 times.

Of course, in order to create and sustain credit bubbles, there must be a seemingly endless supply of debtors. The home owners, margined investors, traders, speculators, businesses, entrepreneurs and others, all of them having the enthusiasm to take on debt in hopes of future profit and enjoyment, all of them reinforcing each others' beliefs and social mood. A great account of this type of phenomenon is captured in Charles Kindleberger's book, *Manias, Panics and Crashes*.

HOW BOOM AND BUST CYCLES AFFECT AMERICANS

We argue that many factors have increased the amplitude of boom and bust cycles that increasingly whipsawed Americans' net worth and employability to a greater extent than in the past. Before these multiple factors are discussed, let's first examine U.S. Gross Domestic Product (GDP) since 1976 to see how economic conditions have affected American citizens' financial condition.

For 3 Decades GDP Growth Has Slowed

We always like to look at trends as percent changes from a year ago, which prevents us from over-reacting to changes during monthly or even quarterly periods and dispenses with seasonal adjustments. Figure 2-8 shows our GDP growing since 1976, but growing at an ever slower growth rate. Although this is a disquieting trend, it is not that surprising. For many years now,

American opinion has been that their children wouldn't do as well economically as their parents. How is this affecting American household net worth?

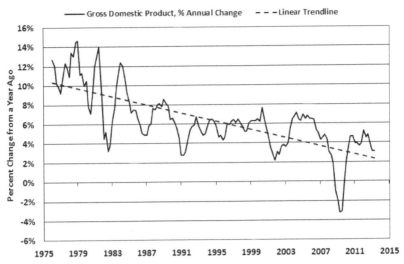

Figure 2-8: Gross Domestic Product (GDP) 1976 – 2013, Percent Change from a Year Ago
Source: St. Louis Federal Reserve Bank

Net Worth Has Suffered

Figure 2-9 illustrates what has happened to U.S. citizens' household net worth and inflation-adjusted household net worth index derived from it. The graph shows that the last two recessions damaged American household net worth. During the previous March to November 2001 recession, nominal U.S. household net worth declined 23.5% and our Great Recession 24.1% from December 2007 to late 2008. Inflation adjusted figures are even worse at 27.03% and 26.93% respectively. During earlier recessionary periods, household net worth actually rose or at its worst lost approximately 5%.

Total household net worth recovered after the 2001 recession and was primarily due to housing prices moving to the stratosphere. In the aftermath of the Great Recession, household net worth has only partially recovered. Household net worth, when adjusted for inflation, is lagging below both the peak in 1999 and the higher peak in 2007.

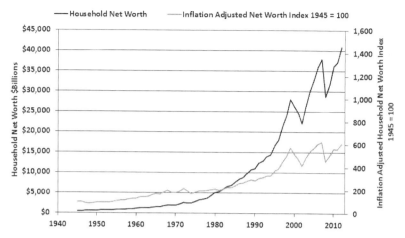

Figure 2-9: U.S. Household Net Worth & Inflation Adjusted Household Net Worth Index 1945 - 2012
Source: Board of Governors of the Federal Reserve System

Employment Falls

The employment picture isn't pretty either. According to Figure 2-10, the percent unemployment rate rose parabolically starting in 2006. The linear trend line shows unemployment drifting up over the decades. The U.S. Bureau of Labor Statistics reported 7 to 8 million lost their jobs due to the 2001 recession. The Great Recession doubled this to 15 or 16 million. Over the last decade, the AFL-CIO estimates that America has lost 2.5 million manufacturing jobs and 850,000+ professional service and information technology jobs overseas. Recessionary job losses, outsourcing of jobs overseas, loss of obsolete jobs and retail job consolidation by megastores such as Walmart or Home Depot have all taken their toll.

Another method for investigating whether or not employment conditions have deteriorated over the decades is to examine the employment recovery duration (time period) it takes for employment to move back to the employment high that occurred around the onset of a recession. In Figure 2-11, the upward linear trend of unemployment since the 1948/1949 recession is clear. The grey area in the last column, representing the Great Recession, is our estimated time required to move back to the previous employment high, which was over 146 million employed.

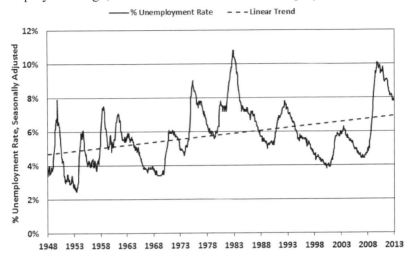

Figure 2-10: Percent Unemployment Rate, Seasonally Adjusted
Source: U.S. Bureau of Labor Statistics

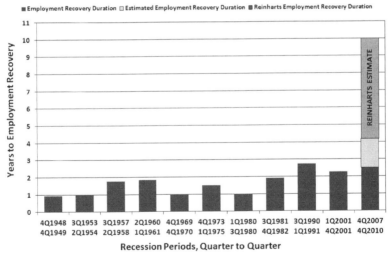

Figure 2-11: Duration of Employment Recovery during Recessions in Years
Source: U.S. Bureau of Labor Statistics

Inspection of the data shows that on average, one half the recovery duration of any recession equals the duration from the peak to trough employment or the duration from trough to recovery duration. A recovery duration of 50 months (4 years, 2 months) is 2 times the duration from the peak employment month, November 2007, to the trough employment month, December 2009. According to the Bureau of Labor Statistics, the U-3 unemployment rate was 4.7% in November 2007, the peak employment month, and 9.9% in December 2009, the trough or lowest employment month. Fifty months translates to January 2012 when U-3 unemployment was 8.3%, which is much higher than November 2007's unemployment rate of 4.7%. Thus, the lack of employment rebound in the Great Recession is unlike all other previous recessions because severe financial crises cause greater economic disruptions.

We believe University of Maryland Professor, Carmen Reinhart, and the American Enterprise Institute's Vincent R. Reinhart clearly show that employment recovery will take much longer than normal in their paper, "After the Fall." The Reinharts studied 15 severe financial crises occurring in both advanced and emerging countries. They found that, in the five advanced economies studied, median unemployment increases were approximately 5% higher. When they looked at the latter advanced countries, pre- and post-crises medians were 2.7% versus 7.9%. Further, they discovered, "In ten of the fifteen post-crisis episodes, unemployment has never fallen back to its pre-crisis level, not in the decade that followed nor through end-2009." At the Kansas City Fed's annual monetary symposium in Jackson Hole, Wyoming, where the Reinharts presented their paper, Carmen Reinhart, during an interview there, stated that an 8% to 9% unemployment rate until 2017 isn't unlikely given the data they have examined. This is five years longer than our previous estimate. If we assume that the Reinharts' conclusions are correct, then Figure 2-11 shows their estimate of employment recovery duration after the last financial crisis, which is longer than in previous periods.[99]

SOCIAL MOOD FACILITATES INFLATION, INTEREST RATES AND GDP

The Inflation Rate, Bond Yields and GDP % Changes Follow in Lockstep

In Figure 2-12 the annual percent change in the inflation rate peaked in 1980 after the 1979 peak GDP percent annual change. A similar phenomenon appears with regard to bond yields. The 10-year US Treasury bond yield peaked in 1982 topping at 14.7% and follows the inflation rate. Bond yields have fallen for 30 years since 1982 along with inflation rates. The shape, duration and time period for these three financial entities: inflation, bond yields and GDP growth rates are all similar. Now let's investigate the relationship between the latter three and ascertain what drives each of them.

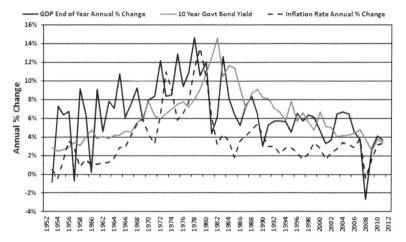

Figure 2-12: GDP vs 10 Year Govt Bond Yield vs Annual Inflation Rate, 1953 to 2012
Source: Bond Yield from Professor Robert Shiller, Annual Inflation Rate from Federal Reserve Bank of Minneapolis, GDP from http://research.stlouisfed.org/ fred2

Social Economic Outlook

Inflation and deflation are facilitated by social economic outlook, which others call herd mentality or which Professor Robert Shiller explains in his book, *Animal Spirits*.[100] The general economic outlook in a society tends to follow the ups and downs of the business cycle. Business cycles are commonly accepted by economists, but they disagree over their causes and composition. Economists do not imply that business cycles are periodic or predictable, but do describe them as fluctuating.

Advocates of the Austrian school of economics theorize that business cycles form because the banking system creates an overexpansion of credit and excessive growth of the money supply causing, in most cases, price and wage inflation. They believe central banks engage in policies that exacerbate unnecessary credit growth and produce booms containing mal-investments, asset bubbles and reduced savings. When the economy can no longer service its debts, credit contracts, bubbles deflate and recessions occur, which corrects the excesses.[101]

Keynesian theories about the causes of business cycles are still the most popular among economists today who use Keynesian concepts to justify government intervention in the economy. British economist, John Maynard Keynes believed that business cycles were caused by aggregate demand variations leading to the ebb and flow of consumption and income levels which in turn led to declining and rising fluctuations in the employment rate. Keynes, in his 1936 *The General Theory of Employment, Interest and Money*, contended that demand rather than supply determined GDP levels. He argued that the government must intervene to increase demand and consumption if an economy was caught in a high unemployment condition.[102]

A less popular theory that is garnering interest is the credit cycle as the origin of business cycles. The concept is that expansion or contraction of private or non-government credit [debt] as a percent of GDP generates booms and busts respectively. Two economists' ideas such as Irving Fisher's debt deflation theory and Hyman Minsky's Financial Instability Hypothesis exemplify this line of thought.[103] We believe the decades-long, credit-fueled, economic boom and the recent Great Recession are powerful arguments for these economists' theories.

Social economic outlook tends to follow the ups and downs of the business cycle described above. As an economic boom and GDP growth progresses, people become confident. Economic surveys report rising consumer confidence. Consumers buy now rather than later because they know prices will be higher in the future. They also borrow more and do so now because they see interest rates rising. As loan demand rises, demand for money can outstrip supply and interest rates increase. When the business cycle turns and the economy sours, consumers reverse behavior, inflation slows, interest rates decline and GDP slows and then declines during recession. Thus consumers have facilitated trends in inflation, interest rates and GDP.[104]

GDP Growth Accelerates, Peaks, Then Slows

You'll notice that after the 1950s, GDP's greatest percent change year over year peaked during year 1979. In other words, GDP tended to rise at an accelerating growth rate from the early 1960s until the end of the 1970s and then GDP grew but at a decelerating growth rate thereafter. The GDP curve in Figure 2-12 is similar to the ones for 10 Year Government Bond Yields and the Inflation Rate.

The previous sections argued that an expansive social economic outlook, expectations of inflation and decades-long growth in credit helped pave the way for GDP increases over the decades. However, several factors have slowed GDP growth rates after 1979.

Richard Duncan, chief economist at Blackhorse Asset Management and author of *The New Depression: The Breakdown of the Paper Money Economy*, details the extraordinary increase of credit for the last 40 years. To accommodate the demand for credit, central banks around the world increased fiat money supplies for over 40 years. Each time an economy would hit a rough patch, another round of money printing and/or lower interest rates was implemented and governments injected fiscal stimuli. The Federal Reserve's Z.1 Flow of Funds Accounts of the United States provides data for Total Credit Market Debt. In 1968, when Congress eliminated the requirement to have gold back up 25% of U.S. currency, the United States Total Credit Market Debt was $1.37 trillion. In 2011, it reached $54.1 trillion or an increase of 40X. Money supply increased by 16.4X. [105] Over time, government debt increased as money supply, credit and stimulus programs increased. As the economic impact of the latter lessened with time and recessions began to take a greater toll on the nation, government authorities tended to increase the size of all of them. Duncan stated, "Every time the economy slowed or a crisis erupted, the Fed cut interest rates or took other steps that encouraged credit expansion and the economy reaccelerated. The reality, however, was that each intervention by the Fed simply created greater distortions throughout the economy as more and more credit was misallocated into unviable investments, or simply wasted on consumption." This chapter's previous section titled "DOES INCREASING GOVERNMENT DEBT EVENTUALLY DECREASE GDP?" reviews several experts' arguments that lowering interest rates, using government spending for the purpose of increasing GDP, increasing taxes and selling U.S. Treasury bonds to pay for the resulting deficits actually decreased GDP growth rates over time. The main argument was that when government siphons money away from private endeavors through taxes and borrowing, it will reduce economic growth and GDP growth rates.[106]

In conclusion, a great deal of direct investment capital was shunted away from wealth-creating businesses and into bonds whose value increases as interest rates decrease. GDP suffered as companies that manufactured goods were deprived of capital. It should not be surprising that GDP growth rates would decline as central banks create vast amounts of liquidity to stimulate their economies. At first this strategy works, but the booms will not last long since they are built upon the pull demand of excess money and not as much on real wealth creation.

Manufacturing Shrinks, Finance Grows

A noticeable transition in the worldwide economic and social changes we've been discussing is the movement of private sector investment and speculative money into finance and real estate and out of manufacturing. Figure 2-13 shows the U.S. manufacturing sector shrinking from 26% of GDP right after World War II to 12% of GDP in 2012. During the same period, the finance, insurance, real estate and rental & leasing sectors moved from 10% to 20%, a doubling of participation. Real-wealth producing companies were progressively starved of private-sector investment money. As their capital dwindled and investment money was withheld and instead invested in government bonds, finance and real estate, these companies didn't know what hit them. The United States had progressively become a service oriented economy whose trade imbalance and current account deficits were exacerbated by losing its manufacturing base. GDP growth rates have inevitably suffered under this phenomenon.

Richard Duncan, author of *The New Depression: The Breakdown of the Paper Money Economy*, also observed this trend during the years from 1964 to 2007. He argues that besides having $50 trillion of credit formation create affluence and wealth over the last few decades, it also switched our economy from a manufacturing base to a services oriented one. Speculative activities increased as easy credit taught investors to purchase assets using other people's money and wait while inflation made them rich. Duncan has coined the word "Creditism" that he believes has replaced capitalism. He explains that the U.S. began using credit to purchase low-cost, foreign manufactured goods after the Bretton Woods system imploded in 1971. The United States' current account deficit ballooned while our manufacturing base declined. The sectors encompassing 1) finance, insurance, real estate, rental and leasing, 2) professional and business services, and 3) education, health care and social assistance have all grown as a percentage of GDP since 1947.[107]

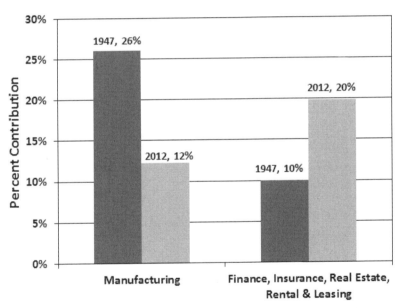

Figure 2-13: Industry Contribution to U.S. Gross Domestic Product
Source: Bureau of Economic Analysis

Many observers believe that American power is waning. A warning sign of this decline is the movement of money and capital from manufacturing to finance. Giovanni Arrighi, Johns Hopkins University Professor, stated in his book, *The Long Twentieth*

Century: Money, Power, and the Origins of Our Times, "In his interpretive scheme, finance capital is not a particular stage of world capitalism, let alone its latest and highest stage. Rather, it is a recurrent phenomenon which has marked the capitalist era from its earliest beginnings in late medieval and early modern Europe." Arrighi described four main periods when a nation or city state became dominant through capitalist development. These were Genoa from the 15th to early 17th century, Holland from the late 16th century through the 18th, Britain from the latter half of the 18th through the early 20th century and the United States from the late 19th into the early 21st century.[108] Arrighi concluded that in each of these four periods, at first, various recurring groupings of government and businesses conducted systemic cycles of [capital] accumulation (SCA). Then as a "built-in limit" was reached, capital accumulation methods shifted from "material expansion" to "high finance" expansion.[109] Arrighi's scholarship and years of study is a powerful argument for this shift to finance in the latter stages of capitalism.

WEALTH DOES NOT PASS THREE GENERATIONS

The heading above is translated from a 2000 year old Chinese proverb, fu bu guo san dai, which warns that the first generation will work hard and live frugally to raise itself above poverty, the second generation will live well from the first's generosity and the third generation will squander whatever is left of the family fortune. Others say that family fortunes can be squandered within two generations. Others believe it is four generations. The early 1600s saying was "rags to riches to rags." A late 19th century Lancashire proverb was "clogs to clogs in three generations." In early 20th century America, the adage was "shirtsleeves to shirtsleeves in three generations." The universality, timelessness and wisdom of this proverb are obvious. Each successive generation tends to lose the work habits and thriftiness of their parents and grandparents. The family grows with each generation and divides and dilutes the family fortune. In economics, if the principle of reversion to the mean is true, then it's true for family members as the original genius and talents of the first generation are diluted with each successive set of descendants and all settle back to average intelligence and talent. And why not apply this proverb, not just to families, but to generations of government bureaucrats, politicians or business leaders. They have all forgotten and/or weren't born when economic crises such as the Great Depression and its lessons were forcibly impressed on its participants.

Thus over many generations, many of us have forgotten our parents' and grandparents' lessons about the financial responsibilities of saving for a rainy day, of avoiding debt, of reusing, repairing and recycling and of living within our means. The American people took on an astonishing amount of debt through home mortgages, home equity loans, credit card debt and all kinds of consumer loans. Personal consumption, financed by debt, grew and finally began contributing to 70% of the U.S. gross domestic product. However, a great deal of the prosperity was an illusion that was financed by debt and not the end result of true wealth creation.

CONCLUSION

Governments have had to ignore the principles of sound money when armed conflict, economic emergencies and high debt levels overtake a nation. The result has been decades of budget deficits and inflation, slowing GDP growth, whipsaw boom and bust cycles, stagnant household net worth, and long-lasting, high unemployment rates. Reformers are studying the deficiencies of national monetary systems and reserve currencies. They are proposing new global monetary systems that may alleviate or prevent some of the worst effects of the current system such as excessive national and global debt, currency wars, trade wars and volatile capital flows. Global monetary system reform is necessary to allow businesses and nations to plan, grow and prosper over the long term.

History teaches us that the power of countries and empires can fade when they evolve from creditor to debtor nation status. Will the United States learn the lessons of history and launch new programs and policies that reinvigorate the nation and initiate another era of wealth creation and prosperity? We believe the difficult but survivable times ahead will show us which policies, lifestyle philosophies, and changes are necessary to insure a bright future for the United States and the rest of the world.

CHAPTER THREE

The Global Debt Crisis

"As long as there is a mountain of debt, the sky will keep falling."

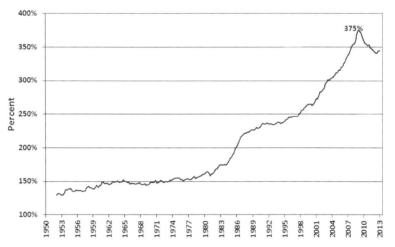

Figure 3-1: U.S. Total Debt as a Percent of Gross Domestic Product
Source: Bureau of Economic Analysis, Federal Reserve

INTRODUCTION

The greatest danger to the United States and the global economy is the massive internal and external debt of highly indebted countries. Figure 3-1, U.S. Total Debt as a Percent of Gross Domestic Product (GDP), shows that the recent 375% ratio surpasses the 1933 value of approximately 300% during the Great Depression. U.S. debt in this figure is total government, business and individual indebtedness.

Those who read the financial news are familiar with the sovereign debt crises of Portugal, Ireland, Italy, Greece and Spain. All these very indebted nations are members of the European Union. Because their currencies are denominated in Euros, they cannot use currency devaluation to pay off their debts. Various economists opine about the likelihood of troubled European nations defaulting on their debt or untethering themselves from the Euro, thus imperiling other nations whose banks and financial institutions could be adversely affected. New York University economics professor Nouriel Roubini believes that International Monetary Fund resources will be inadequate to address Europe's growing debt problems, which he believes will eventually impact the United States and go international.[110]

University of Maryland Professor Carmen Reinhart and Vincent Reinhart at the American Enterprise Institute studied fifteen instances of countries in financial crises similar to the Great Recession. They found that the process of deleveraging, that is, of paying off, defaulting upon or restructuring of loans takes years. Their investigation shows that, in the decade after difficult global financial crises, economies and employment rates grow more slowly.[111] Most economists no longer believe in a quick recovery partially because the debt incurred has been so massive.

We will review the literature about the different types of debt-induced effects such as currency devaluations, sovereign debt defaults and unsupportable government debt service ratios.[112] We'll also examine methods for reducing the debt load and ameliorating the effects of deleveraging.

U.S. GOVERNMENT DEBT

Mary Meeker, a partner at Kleiner Perkins Caufield & Byers, a respected Silicon Valley venture capital firm, has written a February 2011, 266-page report titled, "A Basic Summary of America's Financial Statement," which we highly recommend. Meeker analyzes and details our nation's financial situation as if the federal government were a business. Her evaluation is centered on USA Inc.'s income statement and balance sheet.

The unfunded and underfunded liabilities of the U.S. government are several times larger than its official gross debt of $16+ trillion.

Meeker's figures show that USA Inc.'s fiscal 2010 net worth is -$44.33 trillion. Net entitlement liabilities, which include Social Security, Medicare and disability insurance, are -$30.86 trillion. By comparison, 1966 USA Inc.'s net worth was -$10 trillion. Meeker warns, "Our country is in deep financial trouble. Federal, state and local governments are deep in debt yet continue to spend beyond their means, seemingly unable to stop. Our current path is simply unsustainable." She sets forth several guideposts for setting our country back on the right path. Using only data from readily available public sources and no proprietary ones, Meeker's estimates of assets and liabilities in the balance sheet are on an accrual basis for the next 75 years. Some may pounce on this long period and believe we have plenty of time to reform our financial system. However, many others think change must happen soon. In the following sections, we describe many of the perils that await us far sooner than we'd like.[113]

From one perspective, these unfunded liabilities should actually be called obligations or promises of the U.S. federal government since business accounting liabilities are <u>contractual</u> liabilities. Thus the federal government can reform or cancel many provisions of entitlement programs in order to reduce long run expenses. However, any politicians who attempt substantive reform will likely incur the displeasure of those who constitute many blocks of voters.

Visit http://www.usdebtclock.org/ to view the United States government debt clock.

THE GLOBAL DEBT CRISIS

The United States isn't alone in piling up massive amounts of debt. As shown in Figures 3-2 and 3-4, Japan has the worst government gross debt to GDP ratio. Many European countries also have problematic ratios. In a Bank for International Settlements March 2010 working paper "The future of public debt: prospects and implications," Cecchetti, Mohanty, and Zampolli expressed the opinion, "Our projections of public debt ratios lead us to conclude that the path pursued by fiscal authorities in a number of industrial countries is unsustainable. Drastic measures are necessary to check the rapid growth of current and future liabilities of governments and reduce their adverse consequences for long-term growth and monetary stability." The authors reported that, according to the OECD,[114] total public sector debt of all industrialized countries is set to surpass their entire GDP for 2011. They believe that ageing demographics, high unemployment and low economic growth will insure that paying this enormous debt will be exceedingly difficult.[115]

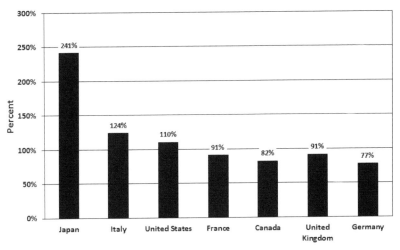

Figure 3-2: Estimated 2013 G-7 Country Government Gross Debt as a Percent of GDP
Source: International Monetary Fund

The authors of the September 2011 Bank for International Settlements article "The real effects of debt," Stephen G. Cecchetti, M. S. Mohanty and Fabrizio Zampolli state that advanced countries have significantly increased their household, non-financial corporate and government indebtedness in the last three decades. Figure 3-3 clearly shows this increase on overall non-financial debt per GDP. In the prior three decades from the 1950s through the 1970s, outstanding debt of U.S. non-financial borrowers as a percent of GDP remained quite steady at or below 150%. The paper's authors use extensive analysis to conclude that many advanced countries with high indebtedness and ageing population must quickly fix their fiscal problems or face slowing economic growth and unsustainable debt.[116]

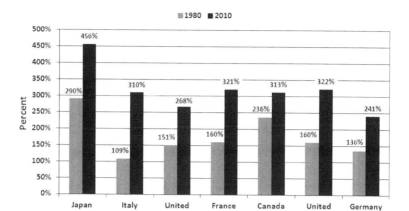

Figure 3-3: Household, Corporate and Government Debt as Percent of Nominal GDP
Source: September 2011 Bank for International Settlements article "The real effects of debt," Stephen G. Cecchetti, M. S. Mohanty and Fabrizio Zampolli, pg 7, (OECD: National Data)

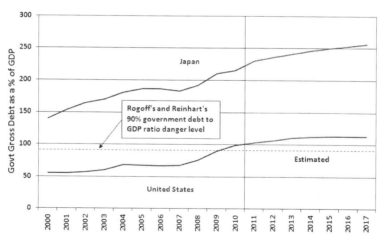

Figure 3-4: Growth of USA and Japanese General Government Gross Debt as a Percent of GDP, 2000 to 2010, Estimated Growth 2011 to 2017
Source: International Monetary Fund[117]

Global debt continues to grow. In Figures 3-4 and 3-5, G-7 country debt accumulation started to accelerate in 2008. The G-7 countries are an economic and political group of the seven largest developed countries and include Japan, the United States, Italy, France,

Canada, the United Kingdom and Germany. The International Monetary Fund estimates that debt growth will continue into the future for the G-7 countries (except for Canada) and for Greece, Ireland, Portugal and Spain.

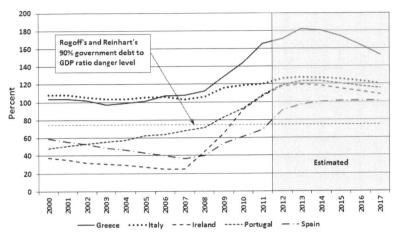

Figure 3-5: G-7 Country General Government Gross Debt as a Percent of GDP, see Figure 3-4 for USA and Japan
Source: International Monetary Fund[118]

Visit website http://www.economist.com/content/global_debt_clock, The Economist magazine's global debt clock. You can check total global government public debt, public debt per person and compare different countries' public debt.

The European Union members: Italy, Spain, Ireland, Greece and Portugal are the focal point for the European sovereign debt crisis. According to the International Monetary Fund, all these countries' general government gross debt as a percent of their GDP started growing at an alarming rate starting in late 2007 to early 2008. European government debt ratings began declining. Credit default swap risk insurance on European country government bonds rose to record price levels. Government to government bond yield spreads widened. Although the European Union and the International Monetary Fund extended multi-billion Euro bailout loans, investors and economists are still worried that the debt crisis will spread to other banks and countries around the world. One of the surest danger signs are swiftly rising yields on government bonds, which implies increasing risk, potential default and a haircut

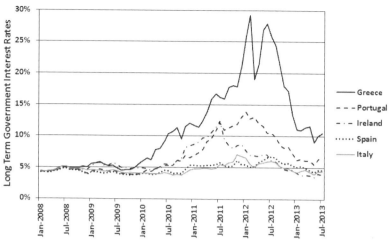

Figure 3-6: European Sovereign Debt Crises: Long Term Government Interest Rates
Source: European Central Bank[119]

or loss on those bonds. In Figure 3-6, the long term government bond interest rates of Greece are symptomatic of the remainder of the troubled peripheral European countries. Austerity programs have been imposed that are aggravating weakening gross domestic products and raising unemployment rates.[120] After mid-2012, interest rates for these countries began dropping in response to the European Central Bank lowering its interest rates, supplying inexpensive loans to European banks to maintain liquidity and on September 6, 2012 announcing the open-ended, limitless purchasing of distressed government bonds of European countries participating in sovereign state bailouts and precautionary programs by the European Financial Stability Facility/ European Stability Mechanism (EFSF/ESM). The European Community, International Monetary Fund, and the European Central Bank have imposed austerity programs as a condition of aid. The combination of austerity and the economic slowdown has resulted in recessions, depression-like conditions and high unemployment in many European Union countries.[121]

DEBT: WHY IT MATTERS

Government Debt per GDP Ratios

In Figures 3-4 and 3-5, the dotted line represents Professors Rogoff's and Reinhart's 90% government debt to GDP ratio above which a country's real government debt tends to increase by 86%, median real GDP growth rates fall by 1%, and average economic growth also drops significantly within three years.[122] Although other analysts believe that debt as a percent of tax revenues is a better indicator of a country's ability to deal with its liabilities, GDP is being used in most calculations. The bigger a country's per-capita GDP, the better that country's situation tends to be. Another criticism is that the United States government's gross debt includes interagency debt while other countries' gross debt doesn't. Thus many people think we should use the United States public debt to GDP ratio value, which is estimated at just above 72.5% as of February 2013. However, the Congressional Budget Office's estimate for future federal government deficits for the next few years is in the trillions of dollars. The CBO's May 2013 estimated debt held by the public at the end of year 2023 is $6.3 trillion. If the federal government public debt or gross debt to GDP ratio continues to grow over the years, the ratio will eventually reach Rogoff's 90% danger level.

Table 3-1: CBO Baseline Projected Federal Government Budget Deficits ($Billions)[123]

Year	2012 Actual	2013	2014	2015	2016	2017
Deficit	-1,087	-642	-560	-378	-432	-482
Year	2018	2019	2020	2021	2022	2023
Deficit	-542	-648	-733	-782	-889	-859

Source: Congressional Budget Office,
http://www.cbo.gov/budget/budget.cfm

Another source supporting Rogoff's and Reinhart's contention that a country's economic growth will slow if its government debt to GDP ratio moves past 90% is the Bank for International Settlements' article "The real effects of debt" authored by Stephen G. Cecchetti, M. S. Mohanty and Fabrizio Zampolli. They relate that, among the 18 OECD advanced countries, the total household, non-financial corporate and government debt to GDP ratio over three decades has climbed inexorably from 167% to 314% in 2010.

The authors conclude that "When public debt is in a range of 85% of GDP, further increases in debt may begin to have a significant impact on growth: specifically, a further 10 percentage point increase reduces trend growth by more than one tenth of 1 percentage point. For corporate debt, the threshold is slightly higher, closer to 90%, and the impact is roughly half as big. Meanwhile for household debt, our best guess is that there is a threshold at something like 85% of GDP, but the estimate of the impact is extremely imprecise." They believe debt problems are worse than they originally thought before starting the article. Because advanced countries' populations are ageing, the social benefits and pensions promised to recipients will cause large increases in government debt and adversely affect economic growth. They suggest solutions. "Maybe we should go further, reducing both direct government subsidies and the preferential treatment debt receives. In the end, the only way out is to increase saving."[124]

In a July 2011 Bloomberg Businessweek article, Rogoff and Reinhart counter arguments by politicians and other pundits that the aforementioned high debt levels aren't necessarily harbingers of debt crises and long-term slow economic growth. The authors contend that only rarely have countries grown their way out of such high debt levels without higher taxation levels and spending cuts. Rogoff and Reinhart also argue that governments tend to absorb problematic private debt and bail out debt-ridden United States' states and municipalities during financial crises. Much of their studies include indebted countries that had fewer and less expensive social benefit programs than we have today with their larger debt loads. The authors assert that countries with over 90 percent of debt to GDP ratios are uncommon and those with greater than 120 percent are even less common. They conjecture that advanced countries are forced to raise tax rates and decrease government expenditures because debt service costs rise as interest rates increase. They conclude that too much debt impedes economic growth.[125]

Rollover Risk

Countries running ever increasing deficits are rolling over debt, or continuously selling new debt issues to replace old debt that is maturing. This tactic of "kicking the can down the road" is likely delaying the inevitable. The rollover risk to pertinent countries is that interest rates could climb suddenly, thus increasing their debt servicing costs, which are repayments of interest and principal. At a certain level, countries may find deficits and total government debt unsustainable. As bond buyers' trust vanishes, causing interest rates to climb higher, governments will struggle to sell their government bonds and contain budgets. As a last resort, indebted countries will contemplate currency devaluation and or debt default.

Several indicators suggest which countries are most in danger of rollover risk. The Economist online magazine has a World Debt Guide, an interactive graphic that presents several countries' debt levels in overall, government, household, financial and non-financial categories. For instance, the Guide shows Japan, Italy, France, Germany, United States and Britain with the highest government debt per GDP. Japan is first on the list with the other countries ranging downward as listed previously. Japan's ratio is currently at 229%+. The Web page's second graphic titled Government Debt Dynamics has a column named "Sovereign debt, years to maturity." The values, which are weight averaged, range from Norway's 2.4 years to Britain's 13.8 years. Those countries with a combination of the highest government debt per GDP and the lowest years to maturity of sovereign debt tend to have high rollover risk such as Japan, Greece, Italy or the United States.[126] For the latter type of countries, long-run inflation requires them to refinance their short term debt at ever increasing interest rates constantly causing debt service costs to escalate quickly.[127]

REDUCING THE DEBT LOAD WILL TAKE TIME

We've shown you the high overall debt to GDP ratios of many nations. So how long will it take to deleverage and get out from under all this private debt so that the global economy can return to some kind of growth and prosperity? Far longer than we'd like. According to University of Maryland Professor Carmen Reinhart and Vincent Reinhart, at American Enterprise Institute, the duration to get back to normal ratios will be seven years. The authors studied 15 financial crises similar to the 2008 meltdown. They outlined their conclusions in an August 2010 National Bureau of Economic Research paper titled, "After the Fall." They found that nations trapped in these crises suffered an approximate 38 percent median decrease in domestic credit per GDP. The 15 nations studied had credit booms lasting approximately 10 years and the deleveraging lasting about the same duration and "often a full decade (and even longer)."[128]

But first let's look at the consumer sector of the economy especially as a typical American citizen would view it.

THE HARD HIT U.S. PRIVATE SECTOR WON'T DELEVERAGE QUICKLY

Unemployment Will Remain High For Years

The Bureau of Labor Statistics reports that the U-3 unemployment rate has steadily declined below the 10% high in October 2008. The BLS's U-3 is defined as the "total unemployed, as a percent of the civilian labor force (official unemployment rate)" and is the rate most often headlined. However, U-3 doesn't fully reveal the jobs situation. The BLS doesn't count as unemployed a large number of discouraged workers who are no longer looking for work. If they were counted, then the unemployment rate would be much higher. For a fuller picture, we should turn to the BLS's U-6 statistic, which is "total unemployed, plus all persons marginally attached to the labor force, plus total employed part time for economic reasons, as a percent of the civilian labor force plus all persons marginally attached to the labor force." U-6 tends to range from 1.7 to 1.9 times larger than U-3.[129]

The number of new jobs must keep up with population growth to eventually return the nation to full employment. The best method for understanding the employment situation is to examine the percent of the population employed over time. In the Figure 3-7, "U.S. Civilian Labor Force Participation as a Percent of Civilian Noninstitutional Population 16 Years and Over," we can visualize how population has increased while the percent of the people employed has decreased significantly over the last decade.

An Organisation for Economic Co-operation and Development (OECD) paper titled "Small Businesses, Job Creation and Growth: Facts, Obstacles and Best Practices" concluded that 'SMEs (small and medium-sized enterprises) account for 60 to 70 percent of jobs in most OECD countries, with a particularly large share in Italy and Japan, and a relatively smaller share in the United States. Throughout, they also account for a disproportionately large share of new jobs, especially in those countries which have displayed a strong employment record, including the United States and the Netherlands.'[130] "SMEs" then are one of the most important factors in job creation or destruction. As SMEs' or small businesses' fortunes rise and fall, so does the American employment situation.

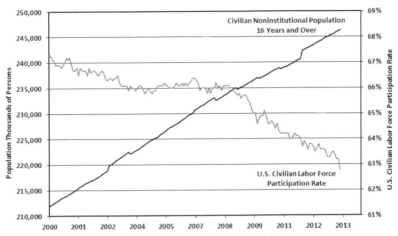

Figure 3-7: U.S. Civilian Labor Force Participation as a Percent of Civilian Noninstitutional Population 16 Years and Over
Source: Federal Reserve Bank of St. Louis, Fredgraph: Civilian Labor Force Participation Rate (CIVPART) and Civilian Noninstitutional Population (CNP16OV)

Intuit, a small business products and services corporation, provides an online Small Business Employment Index using a database collected from 70,000 small businesses having fewer than 20 employees. According to the Bureau of Labor Statistics, this subset of smallest businesses employs almost 20 million and encompasses 87% of all U.S. private employers. Figure 3-8 shows that small business employment fared worse than national employment and is experiencing the same slow recovery path as mentioned in the previous paragraphs. The National Business Employment Index dropped only 5.96% peak to trough due to the latest recession. The Small Business Employment Index declined 7.00% peak to trough, which is worse than the national employment figures. Both Indices haven't recovered to their previous highs.

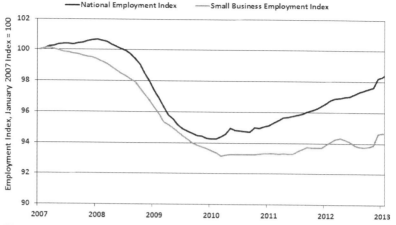

Figure 3-8: Intuit Business Employment Indexes
Source: Intuit, Inc., Intuit Small Business Indexes, http://index.intuit.com/

The State of U.S. Consumer Personal Saving Rates

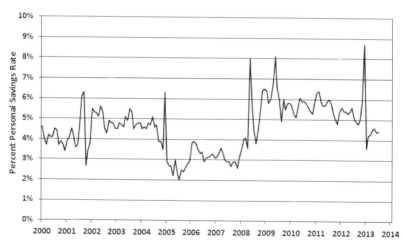

Figure 3-9: Personal Saving Rate, Percent, Monthly, Seasonally Adjusted Annual Rate
Source: Federal Reserve Bank of St. Louis

U.S. consumers are saving more and feeling more pessimistic than compared to the last decade's averages—warning us of less than positive consumption forecasts. The stressed consumers' personal savings rate has risen from 0.8% in April 2005 to 4.4% in July 2013. Consumers' increased frugality was assisted by lending institutions' withdrawal of credit. Homeowner's equity lines of credit, HELOCs, have been canceled. Lenders have tightened their lending standards. Credit card companies have cancelled accounts or lowered credit limits. Thus consumers experienced the same credit contraction that businesses were living through. From 2011 to July 2013, consumers were decreasing their savings rate and increasing their credit obligations as unemployment, underemployment and declining wages adversely affected their standard of living.

Will Rising Consumer Credit Rescue the U.S. Economy?

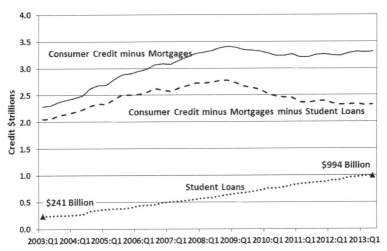

Figure 3-10: Consumer Credit (Excludes Mortgages) minus Student Loans $trillions
Source: Federal Reserve Bank of New York

Many analysts studying post-2011 U.S. consumer credit data from the Federal Reserve Bank of New York have concluded that an economic turnaround is at hand. A 14% drop in mortgage debt shows deleveraging in that sector has been continuing. Under normal circumstance, that would free up more discretionary income and stimulate an economy whose GDP is 70% consumption. The consumer credit minus mortgage debt curve demonstrates this in Figure 3-10. However, if we subtract the burgeoning student loan values from the former, another picture emerges. Student loans have increased from $241 billion from 2003 to $994 Billion to 2nd quarter 2013, a 4 times increase. A whole generation of students have indebted themselves to such an extent that it may take years to extricate themselves. Many, finding employment opportunities poor and wages stagnating, will have to curtail expenditures. These debt sectors: mortgage debt, home equity lines of credit, auto loans and credit cards are down from their previous highs. While student loans are up 74.8% since 2000. Consumers haven't deleveraged nearly enough to weather another economic setback in the future.[131]

To summarize, the combination of sluggish employment recovery, lackluster small business hiring outlook and a negative social economic outlook continues to slow both economic recovery and debt liquidation.

POSSIBLE DEBT CRISIS SCENARIOS

Sovereign Debt Default

The Congressional Budget Office's estimated United States' federal budget deficits to 2021 lead many alarmists to believe the U.S. could default on its debts just as other nations have. However Ellen Brown, author of *Web of Debt*, informed readers that the U.S. isn't subject to debt defaults. Brown opines, "Unlike Greece and other EU members, which are forbidden to issue their own currencies or borrow from their own central banks, the U.S. government can solve its debt crisis by the simple expedient of either printing the money it needs directly, or borrowing it from its own central bank, which prints the money. The current term of art for this maneuver is 'quantitative easing,' and Ferguson says it is what has so far 'stood between the US and larger bond yields' -"[132]

However the United States has defaulted on its debt in the past. The first was in 1790 when the U.S. defaulted on both its external and domestic debt. Another occurred in 1933 when the federal government defaulted on its domestic debt by swapping U.S. citizens' gold for paper dollars and then revaluing the dollar to gold conversion ratio to its citizens' disadvantage. In 1971 President Nixon closed the dollar to gold conversion window to other nations, which was a de facto external debt default.[133]

Could the U.S. pile on debt for the next twenty years as the Japanese have with their 230%+ government public debt to GDP ratio? This is unlikely since Japan financed their debt with

Japanese savings while the U.S. must borrow from the world. Eventually the bond vigilantes may finally have their way, withdraw from the U.S. debt market causing high bond interest rates, which could cause unsustainable debt servicing costs.

Professors Kenneth Rogoff and Carmen Reinhart, in a 2011 NBER paper "This Time is Different: A Panoramic View of Eight Centuries of Financial Crises," used a newly compiled historical database to show the following: "Aside from the current lull, one element that jumps out from the figure is the long periods where a high percentage of all countries are in a state of default or restructuring. Indeed, it shows five pronounced peaks or default cycles. The first is during the Napoleonic War while the most recent cycle encompasses the emerging market debt crises of the 1980s and 1990s." Their paper is a warning that our recent financial crisis is similar to those in the past, that it may unfold in the same manner and that "serial default remains the norm."[134]

Most of the financial headlines concentrate on the probability of European countries defaulting on their debt. The stronger members of the European Union and the International Monetary Fund will likely bail out troubled countries only if the banks accept major "haircuts" on their holdings of relevant government bonds. The latter's deep reduction in value could lead to financial turmoil and global contagion. Some analysts are warning of possible social unrest greater than what we have seen so far. Each nation's scenario could be slightly different, but the general way the drama could play out will be similar in most cases.

Using Currency Devaluation to Reduce Government's Debt Load

The Federal Reserve Bank of New York defines devaluation as the deliberate downward adjustment in the official exchange rate, which reduces the currency's value with respect to other countries' value. In this debt burdened era as in others, nations devalue their currencies to avoid defaulting on part or all of their debt. The theory is that debt will be easier to retire with a currency cheaper relative to other currencies. However whether a country chooses currency devaluation or government debt default, the marketplace will raise that country's bond rates and rating agencies will be inclined to cut that country's credit rating. Devaluation also tends to decrease imports and increase exports thus reducing trade deficits. It can produce inflation, making goods more expensive for its citizens and decrease economic growth. In retaliation, other nations may competitively devalue, in a "beggar thy neighbor" fashion, to aid their exporting industries that are being adversely affected by other nations' devalued currencies. Essentially each country engaging in currency devaluation is attempting to bolster its own industries to grow its way out of poor economic conditions, but at the expense of other countries.[135] Thus, currency wars are trade wars in disguise and could intensify any future political, social or economic instability.

Debt-burdened European peripheral countries are contemplating leaving the Euro, adopting back their local currencies, and devaluing to lighten their government debt load. As we have written in the previous paragraph, this currency devaluation is a classic maneuver that doesn't necessarily succeed. The magazine Der Spiegel examines what they call, "the catastrophic consequences of a crash of the euro." Der Speigel's quotation below is only a small part of what could happen if a significant number of countries ditched the euro.

"Everything that has grown together in two decades of euro history would have to be painstakingly torn apart. Millions of contracts, business relationships and partnerships would have to be reassessed, while thousands of companies would need protection from bankruptcy. All of Europe would plunge into a deep recession. Governments, which would be forced to borrow additional billions to meet their needs, would face the choice between two unattractive options: either to drastically increase taxes or to impose significant financial burdens on their citizens in the form of higher inflation."[136]

The Speigel staff believes the European Community Bank, which has been able to prop up the euro through huge monetary bailouts, has nearly reached the limits of their reserves. Any more purchases of sovereign debt could trigger even larger interest rate increases. If countries begin abandoning the euro, Swiss bank Credit Suisse reports that some European banks could "come to a standstill." Many would suffer total capital deficits in the hundreds of billions of euros. Der Spiegel opines that this scenario among others they describe is "so frightening" European leaders should arrive at some agreement without delay. Instead, Eurozone governments are becoming polarized on euro policy matters.[137]

Could European countries discard the euro, return to their old currencies and follow the scenarios that Der Spiegel and its many sources envision in their magazine article? Many pundits think it unlikely, but analyzing the consequences of Euro dissolution is a sobering exercise nonetheless.

The End of the Debt Supercycle

Economic analyst John Mauldin, in his *Thoughts From The Frontline* newsletter, believes, as we do, that most of the developed countries are nearing the end of what he calls the "Debt Supercycle." Many individuals have contributed to this latter idea, which Mauldin defines as a "decades-long growth of debt from small and easily-dealt-with levels, to a point where bond markets rebel and the debt has to be restructured or reduced and/or a program of austerity must be undertaken to bring the debt back to manageable proportions." Greece, as an example, is near the end of their Debt Supercycle having defaulted on their debt in March 2012 thus triggering over $3 billion of credit default swaps settlements. Mauldin believes in the possibility that the United States will reach this end point or "End Game" as he calls it, when it moves beyond the point where the federal government can't keep running deficits of 10% of GDP forever.[138][139] The end of the "Debt Supercycle" may take many years to arrive or could land on our collective doorsteps very quickly.

The United States and many of the other advanced nations experienced a 1920s credit boom, which a number of economists argue was the catalyst for or a large contributor to the Great Depression of the 1930s. Credit in the United States during the 1920s was fueled by three economic sectors: real estate, Wall Street and consumer durables.[140] Economist Ludwig von Mises, a proponent of the Austrian school of economics and classical liberalism, no doubt observed and studied this phenomenon and wrote in his 1949 book, *Human Action*, "The wavelike movement affecting the economic system, the recurrence of periods of boom which are followed by periods of depression, is the unavoidable outcome of the attempts, repeated again and again, to lower the gross market rate of interest by means of credit [debt] expansion.

There is no means of avoiding a final collapse of a boom brought about by credit [debt] expansion. The alternative is only whether the crisis should come sooner as a result of a voluntary abandonment of further credit [debt] expansion or later as a final and total catastrophe of the currency system involved." Subsequent history shows central banks repeatedly lowering interest rates and increasing debt to smooth out the business cycle just as Ludwig von Mises had written. Rather than abandoning the creation of more debt, governments have embraced it during and after the last period of financial crises. If Ludwig von Mises' words of wisdom prove accurate, then we will eventually witness, as the end result of a decades-long global credit boom, a Mauldin-like "End Game," with an international financial system in crisis.[141]

When Will The Bond Vigilantes Strike?

According to Wikipedia, a bond vigilante is a "bond market investor who protests monetary or fiscal policies they consider inflationary by selling bonds, thus increasing yields." In a CNBC-TV interview, New York University professor and economist Nouriel Roubini stated, "If you keep on having trillion dollar deficits, this year, next year, the following year, before there's going to be any change, then at some point you need the discipline of the bond market vigilantes. The trigger could be a fiscal crisis in the U.S. states. ...The fiscal path in the United States is clearly unsustainable. The sovereign debt problems are an issue in the peripheral Eurozone, but we have large budget deficits in the U.S., in the U.K., in Japan. The U.S. is doing less than anybody else."[142]

Imagine you are a government bond holder. First you learn government bonds are those issued by a country in its own currency and that sovereign bonds are issued by a country in a foreign currency. The United States issues U.S. Treasury government bonds designated in its own currency, the dollar. Greece is an example of a nation that issues sovereign bonds in Euros rather than in their former national currency, the drachma. Government bonds are supposed to be free of risk because the issuing country can levy taxes and/or print money to back the bonds. Sovereign bonds are generally assumed more at risk because their countries are unable to "print" foreign currency.[143]
However, government bonds, as we have defined them, are subject to several risks. The first risk is that countries issuing government

bonds have defaulted or restructured their debt in the past leaving bond holders with "haircuts," wherein only a portion of the bonds' value was paid back. The second risk is that foreign bond holders may lose value on their bonds due to adverse foreign exchange rates. The third risk is that countries may devalue their currencies so they can pay their debts more easily. However, devaluation decreases the value of their government bonds. As an example, central banks inject electronically created money into their economy and foreign economies by providing low interest rate loans or by purchasing financial assets from the private sector and banks. Bond holders understand that, to their detriment, such programs can be very inflationary. Market historians know that in a fiat-money and credit-based economy, bond holders must have trust in the government to pay them back at a reasonable rate. Once trust is breached—and no one really knows when that will happen—the bond vigilantes will have their day and bond prices will decline very fast.[144]

In "Debt Overhangs: Past and Present," Carmen M. Reinhart, Vincent R. Reinhart and Kenneth Rogoff studied 26 instances of government debt per GDP surpassing 90% for over five years. The average length of the all 26 debt overhangs was approximately 23 years, over two decades. Twenty of the twenty-six persisted over ten years. The authors discovered that "real interest rates were either lower or about the same as during the lower debt/GDP years." The real interest rate is approximately the nominal interest rate minus the inflation rate. They concluded, "Those waiting for financial markets to send the warning signal through higher interest rates that government policy will be detrimental to economic performance may be waiting a long time." Thus the bond vigilantes may be held in abeyance for many more years than many realize.[145]

DERIVATIVES MAY INTENSIFY ANY SOVEREIGN DEBT CRISES

According to Wikipedia: "A derivative is a broad term covering a variety of financial instruments whose values are derived from one or more underlying assets, market securities or indices." The total notional value of the global derivatives market is enormous. Depending on which analyst or organization one takes their figures from, the peak value of the global derivatives market was estimated at $683 trillion to $1,000 trillion in 2008. In comparison, Global

GDP is \$60 trillion. But notional amounts are used to calculate payments by all parties of a derivatives contract and are misleading because notional amounts normally aren't exchanged. Another smaller measure, gross market value is the cost of replacing all open derivative contracts at prevailing market prices. For instance, for June 2012, the total notional amount of global derivatives according to the Bank for International Settlements (BIS) was \$638.9 trillion, but its gross market value was \$25.4 trillion. According to the BIS, the best measure is gross credit exposure, which is "gross market value after taking into account legally enforceable bilateral netting agreements." The latter is just a matter of consolidating all derivatives contracts that directly offset each other. At December 2011, gross credit exposure was \$3.7 trillion, which is still a very large number.[146] However, even though netting and gross credit exposure calculations apparently shrink the risk of a financial system meltdown, observers warn us that derivatives market participants could be badly mauled by a "Euroland" breakup that some believe could be the worst financial crisis the world has ever seen.[147]

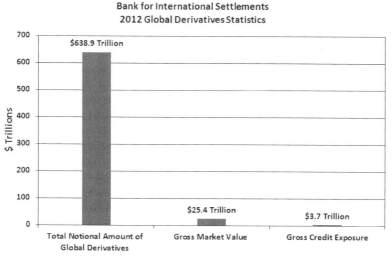

Figure 3-11: Bank for International Settlements 2012 Global Derivatives Statistics
Source: Bank for International Settlements, "OTC derivatives market activity in the second half of 2012," available at
http://www.bis.org/statistics/derstats.htm

Four Investment Banks Own Most of the U.S. Banking Industry's Derivatives

The Office of the Comptroller of the Currency states in their "OCC's Quarterly Report on Bank Trading and Derivatives Activities Third Quarter 2012" that the "Four large commercial banks represent 93.2% of the total banking industry notional amounts and 81% of industry net current credit exposure." Those four large investment banks are Goldman Sachs, JPMorgan Chase, Bank of America and Citibank. Since the notional amount of derivatives held by all insured commercial banks and savings associations in the U.S. totals $227 trillion, these four large banks own about $211 trillion of derivatives or a little less than one third of total global derivative contracts as calculated by the Bank for International Settlements. The concentration of derivatives held by the "too-big-to-fail" banks is troubling. For instance, interest rate derivatives comprise 81% of the notional amounts of all derivatives. If the European debt crisis worsens suddenly and interest rates rise rapidly, then any bank or group of banks with too great a one-sided interest rate derivatives bet could find itself in trouble.[148]

COUNTERVAILING TRENDS AND POSSIBLE DEBT SOLUTIONS

Emerging Countries' Countervailing Economic Trends

Many emerging countries have spent the last 10 to 15 years amassing international reserves and paying down their debt while western nations were doing the opposite. In fact, many of them encountered overly strong economic growth leading to significant inflation. Thus their financial situation has allowed much greater decision making power to counter the slowing growth of indebted advanced nations.[149] Many of these countries have young, growing populations that foretell of economic growth in contrast to the aging populations of advanced countries that signal decreased consumption.

The emerging countries have been recovering from the Great Recession much faster than the western nations. Their current problem is to insulate themselves from the West's vulnerabilities of massive debt, sluggish growth and decreasing or lower than expected consumption. As many of them are exporting countries, they may fiscally stimulate to increase internal consumption and mitigate the effects of declining exports. This would help the advanced countries by lowering the latter's trade deficits and decreasing the emerging countries' international reserves. Some of the emerging countries, however, may engage in currency devaluation to protect their export trade and capital controls to influence the flow of money into and out of their countries.[150]

Prolonging the European Debt Crisis

The European debt crisis has spawned a number of lending and assistance programs designed to issue debt for the recapitalization of Eurozone countries' lenders who require financial stabilization or help with sovereign debt problems. In 2010, the European Union created the European Financial Stability Facility (EFSF), which has capital guarantees of hundreds of billions of euros from other Eurozone countries.[151][152] So far EFSF has extended aid through the European Financial Stability Mechanism (EFSM) program to Cyprus, Greece, Hungary, Ireland, Latvia, Portugal, Romania, and Spain. As of 2012, bailouts have totaled over €470 billion. In 2013, the EFSF's assistance program will expire. In September 2012, the European Financial Stability Facility and the European Financial Stability Mechanism was replaced by the European Stability Mechanism (ESM), which will be able to lend a maximum of €500 billion.[153] Economist John Mauldin in his Thoughts from the Frontline newsletter estimates that the bailout costs of troubled European countries will be €3 trillion. Boston Consulting Group suggests €6 trillion will be required.[154] Thus all of the bailout and lending facilities may only be an instrument for "kicking the can down the road," that is, of delaying the chaos of debt default, currency turmoil and market volatility. Others believe that they will allow the European Community time to pay off, reduce or renegotiate debt.

U.S. Deleveraging Trends

State and local governments, which have to balance their budgets, have been belatedly decreasing their debt levels since the second quarter of 2010. However, the federal government has shown a steep increase in public debt as it attempts to stimulate the U.S. economy and simultaneously grapple with ongoing budget deficits.

Individuals and families have been deleveraging through debt payoffs, bankruptcies and home foreclosures. Individuals are going through this deleveraging process faster than in other nations. Thus it is not surprising that the U.S. economy, though experiencing slow growth, is doing better than other countries especially those trapped in the European debt crisis.

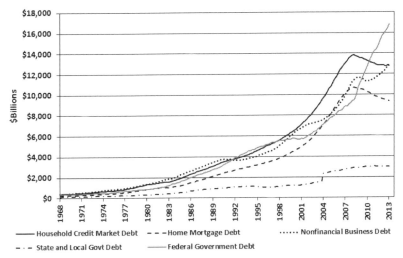

Figure 3-12: U.S. Selected Sector Debt
Source: Federal Reserve Economic Data

The housing market is clearing itself of the speculative price increases from the 1990s and 2000s. The latest Case/Shiller Home Price Index shows average home prices increasing for both the 10- and 20-City Composites. It's too soon to say that a residential real estate bottom has arrived, but many analysts are optimistic.

In hindsight, anyone looking at Professor Robert Shiller's 1890 to present house price index would intuitively understand that the unprecedented and incredible 83% parabolic price rise from 1997 to 2006 could not go on forever. We know that what goes up must ultimately come down. This innate knowledge is embodied in the economic principle known as "reversion to the mean." In the case of house prices reverting back to the mean and becoming affordable again, we can surmise from Figure 3-13 that prices could fall back to or undershoot below the U.S. home price mean. In a Yahoo Finance interview, Professor Shiller didn't necessarily see a housing bottom or that there would be a turnaround in prices.

He opined that home prices have momentum, that is, if the trend is down, then they'll tend to keep going down. Shiller questioned whether house prices would overshoot below the mean, which he stated has often occurred after market bubbles. Shiller said that price-to-income and price-to-rent ratios have declined a lot. He wasn't sure where those means were, but was confident that we weren't overpriced any longer.[155] Professor Shiller's data and opinion coincides with our own that markets must rid themselves of the parabolic price spikes often caused by excessive and euphoric speculation.

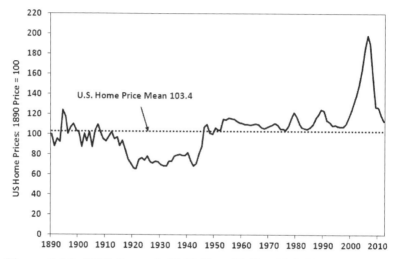

Figure 3-13: 1890 through 2012 Case/Shiller U.S. Home Prices
Source: Online Data Robert Shiller,
http://www.econ.yale.edu/~shiller/data.htm

Foreclosures are the main process driving debt reduction for individuals and families. As home prices are inexorably lowered, homes will become more affordable, the housing market will recover, personal consumption will increase and all will return to the mean.

Reinhart Describes How "Financial Repression" Can Liquidate Government Debt

Professor Carmen Reinhart and M. Belen Sbrancia, in their March 2011 NBER article "The Liquidation of Government Debt," explain how the United States and Great Britain liquidated their

WWII debt through "Financial repression [that] includes directed lending to government by captive domestic audiences (such as pension funds), explicit or implicit caps on interest rates, regulation of cross-border capital movements, and (generally) a tighter connection between government and banks." They further write, "Low nominal interest rates help reduce debt servicing costs while a high incidence of negative real interest rates liquidates or erodes the real value of government debt. Thus, financial repression is most successful in liquidating debts when accompanied by a steady dose of inflation." [156]

Reinhart and Sbrancia conclude that the United States and other countries might begin to use "financial repression" policies. Some countries are already doing so. Since the United States is a sovereign nation able to print its own money, the federal government is able to keep government bond yields low. They have, to this point, been unable to create enough inflation, but that may change as the economy improves. Anyone buying government bonds would effectively be levied a hidden tax. Debt liquidation will take many years, partially because present day debt includes vast amounts of individual and corporate debt, which contrasts to WWII debt that resided mainly with government while the private sector had deleveraged during the Great Depression. [157]

Carrying out a financial repression policy could be short circuited if trust in their government bonds evaporates so that government bond yields rise significantly above the inflation rate. Governments could also overspend thus increasing their debt load and slowing debt liquidation. The U.S presently doesn't have as large a manufacturing base and ready markets as compared to the WWII era. We also have high unemployment and a higher debt to GDP ratio. The great question will be whether or not countries could successfully carry out financial repression over a long period of time.

CONCLUSION

Over the last few decades, advanced countries in all sectors of their societies have incurred record levels of debt whether in absolute amounts or as ratios of debt to GDP, consumer income or tax revenues. We cannot ignore the dangers inherent in such massive global debt. When all countries abandoned gold-backed money and began to depart from sound monetary principles, governments inflated their money supplies and intervened in their economies with little restraint. Fiat money backed the creation of enormous quantities of credit [debt]. For instance, over four decades, United States credit expanded 40X, far larger than the 16X money supply growth. There is little difference between money and credit except the latter would pay interest. Whether one took dollar bills or a credit instrument, such as a U.S. Treasury bond that paid interest, and requested that the Treasury give you your money back, they would hand back dollars in either case. Many economic theories tended to be based on the manipulation and size of the money supply and downplayed or misunderstood the massive role of credit in the economy. When businesses' and individuals' income could no longer service the increasing level of debt, a credit freeze and financial crisis struck in 2008. As we have mentioned before, because the global economy is still frail and debt has not been dealt with, another crisis is most likely brewing and may surprise most people who believe a slow but steady recovery is in the works.

In this chapter, we have written about some of the possible debt crisis scenarios that could occur. In the next chapter we will describe in more detail the chances for deflation, inflation or hyperinflation, for general economic possibilities such as recession, stagflation or depression, and for different types of government intervention that will influence all of the former. The framework for discussion, in the next chapter, will be the writings of Ray Dalio at Bridgewater Associates, an investment management company. His perceptive February 2012 article, "An In-Depth Look at Deleveragings ©," takes into account government intervention. We will also lean heavily on Richard Duncan's theories as detailed in his book, *The New Depression: The Breakdown of the Paper Money Economy*. Depending on what governments around the world do, but especially what the U.S. and the Eurozone does, the outcomes for the economy could range broadly from lackluster to catastrophic.

CHAPTER FOUR

Looking Ahead:
Possible Macroeconomic Scenarios

"The only function of economic forecasting is to make astrology look respectable." – John Kenneth Galbraith

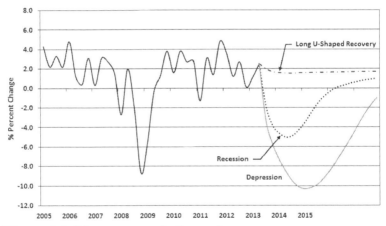

Figure 4-1: Macroeconomic Scenarios
Courtesy: U.S. Department of Commerce, Bureau of Economic Analysis

INTRODUCTION

Although this century's economic problems shook our confidence, the nation will eventually recover and life will go on. As we look ahead, our first order of business is to strive for objectivity and analysis. Remember that no one has a crystal ball foretelling which macroeconomic scenario will become reality and we don't claim to have one either. First we will describe how government intervention could shape and influence which macroeconomic scenarios the country and the global economy may follow. Next we'll review the various arguments and theories that experts and organizations have about different macroeconomic scenarios and their chances for emerging. Within each of these scenarios, we will review the prospects for inflation, disinflation, stagflation, deflation and hyperinflation.

We believe that government intervention will have the greatest role in shaping the various macroeconomic scenarios their countries will follow. Since all countries now use fiat (paper) money with its accompanying ability to create vast amounts of credit, their governments can undertake fiscal stimuli and monetary policy on a global basis at levels greater than ever imagined by previous eras' economists.

THE ROLE OF GOVERNMENT INTERVENTION

Perhaps the best description of how governments will deal with their massive debt and how that will affect their economies is given by Ray Dalio and his analysts at Bridgewater Associates (http://www.bwater.com/) in a paper titled, "An In-Depth Look at Deleveragings ©." Deleveraging involves decreasing the ratio of debt to income. According to Dalio there are ugly deflationary, and beautiful and ugly inflationary deleveragings and these results are determined by the quantity and speed of "1) debt reduction, 2) austerity, 3) transferring wealth from the haves to the have-nots and 4) debt monetization." First, if governments manage this process poorly, then the process becomes an "ugly deflationary deleveraging," an overly fast pace of defaulting or restructuring debt and too much austerity that devastates debtors, produces deflation, collapses investment confidence and, when extreme enough, induces a deflationary depression such as the 1930-1932 Great Depression. Their societies may fare badly with social upheavals and, in some cases, military conflicts. Second, if done well with a "beautiful deleveraging," then governments print money, monetize debt and devalue their currencies just enough to offset the forces of deflation and provide positive economic growth. Dalio considers the 2008-Present U.S. deleveraging as an example of "beautiful deleveraging." Third, if there is too much money printing/debt monetization and too great a devaluation of the currency, then an "ugly inflationary deleveraging" can occur. In the extreme, it produced, as a Dalio example, Germany's Weimar

Republic 1918-1923 hyperinflation leaving its currency essentially worthless and its economy in shambles.[158] The difference between Dalio's study and others of its type is his quantification of financial variables such as GDP, bond yields, debt levels, or inflation figures from actual historical deleveraging parallels to illustrate and help verify his arguments. Dalio's paper supports our opinion that government policies will be the major factor shaping future macroeconomic scenarios.

In his paper, Dalio divides the United States' Great Depression into two parts, an "ugly deflationary deleveraging" from 1930 to1932, the first phase, and a "beautiful deleveraging" from 1933 to 1937, the second phase. The first phase was an "ugly deflationary depression" when economic activity declined swiftly, the debt to income ratio rose rapidly, credit levels fell deeply and the stock market collapsed. During the second phase, appropriate amounts of money printing commenced in 1933 and the dollar to gold convertibility ratio was changed from $20.67 to $35 in 1934 devaluing the dollar by 40%. The ensuing reflation resulted in greater economic activity and rising GDP.[159]

There are multiple possible causes for the Great Depression: a margin-fueled stock market boom and bust, monetary policy mistakes, a restrictive gold standard and European government debt crises. Since most economists argue the Great Recession was the result of too much debt (credit) and eventually too little income to pay for it, the often ignored 1920s credit boom that preceded the Great Depression is being revisited. As an example, Eichengreen and Mitchener contend in their article "The Great Recession as a credit boom gone wrong" that expanding credit played a much greater role in boosting economic activity beyond normal, creating consumer euphoria and fostering investor mania. During the 1920s, lenders vied to provide ever greater amounts of household credit, which resulted in the ratio of consumer debt to individual income doubling from 1918-1920 to 1929. Americans were buying new cars using credit structured as installment payments for almost 67% of new cars by 1927. Throughout the 1920s, increasing numbers of consumers used installment plans to pay for appliances, furniture, clothing, pianos, and radios. Technological innovations such as radio, automotive advances and labor saving appliances whet the appetite of a burgeoning American consumerism. Most historians know about the role of the early 1920s Florida real estate boom.[160]

Fewer of them have written about the office building boom and the commercial mortgage-backed securities that financed U.S. skyscraper construction in the 1920s. By 1925, their issuance, which led to overbuilding and subsequent vacancies, was 23% of total U.S. corporate debt. In 1934 issuance dropped to 0.14% and then quickly disappeared. William Goetzmann and Frank Newman ("Securitization in the 1920s") assert that these 1920s real estate bonds were just as deadly for the 1930s economy as the mortgage-backed securities were in the present era's Great Recession.[161]

These facts illustrate many of the similarities between the credit boom (debt buildup) of the 1920s and the growth of debt leading up to the credit freeze and financial system meltdown of the 2007-2009 Great Recession. In addition, the ratio of U.S. household debt to GDP was at a record high of 98% in 2007 having climbed steeply from the 1940s. In 1929, the ratio rose to 70% and increased further to nearly 100% by 1933.[162]

The manner in which the U.S. government responded produced an "ugly deflationary deleveraging" expressed as a deflationary depression from 1930 to 1932 and a "beautiful deleveraging" generating a brief price deflation followed by stagflation during the 2007-2009 Great Recession. However, when we analyze differences between the 1930-1932 Great Depression and the 2007-2009 Great Recession, they may not bode well for the United States economy going forward even though Dalio judged the "2008-Present U.S. Deleveraging" as a "beautiful deleveraging." For instance, the U.S. Total Debt as a Percent of Gross Domestic Product (GDP) ratio at the end of 1929 was 175% and in 2007 it was 354%, twice as large. U.S. total debt is comprised of household, corporate, financial, government sponsored enterprises, and government sector debt. Another indicator is the percent increase in the ratio of U.S. Federal gross debt to gross domestic product (GDP). Gross Federal debt is all of the debt owed by the U.S. Federal government comprised of the debt held by the public and debt owed between Federal government agencies. The Federal gross debt to GDP in 1929 was 16.3% and in 2007 it was 63.8%, a nearly four times multiple. Many European countries had high levels of debt following World War I. By contrast today's European sovereign debt crises may be more dangerous to the financial system than in the 1920s. According to SNL Financial, for the 3rd quarter 2012, leverage ratios as a percent for these large

European banks are Royal Bank of Scotland (UK) 6.45%, Barclays (UK) 4.71%, UBS AG (Switzerland) 4.53%, Credit Suisse (Switzerland) 4.5% and Nordea Bank (Sweden) 4.26%. Average American bank leverage is safer at 12 to 1. For the same period, the six largest U.S. banks' leverage ratios are Wells Fargo 9.4%, Bank of America 7.84%, Citigroup 7.39%, JPMorgan Chase 7.08%, Goldman Sachs 7.17% and Morgan Stanley 7.18%. Generally speaking a leverage ratio is Tier 1 capital divided by tangible assets less derivative liabilities wherein Tier 1 capital is a measure of a bank's financial strength consisting primarily of common stock and disclosed reserves (or retained earnings. Thus United States large banks' higher leverage ratios are a sign of greater financial strength than the European large banks.[163]

The large disparity in debt levels between the two different eras is disturbing because today's massive global debt means greater instability and a longer deleveraging period. In the American political arena, legislative stalemate, ongoing deficit spending and a Wall Street Occupy type of revolt may lead to reactive austerity, withdrawal of financial stimuli and/or a harmful change in Federal Reserve leadership and policy. Dalio may have to divide the present economically troubling times the way he did for the Great Depression except in the opposite order.

Did the Federal Government Prevent a Depression?

At this point the U.S. GDP growth rate should be 5% rather than the anemic rates we've seen since the Great Recession ended. Naturally the federal government knows that real GDP growth rate should be higher and is worried. However the Federal government in concert with the Federal Reserve Bank likely prevented the United States from entering a depression through massive bailouts and creative monetary policy decisions. The following paper reviews how federal government spending buoyed up the economy and lifted many economic indicators.

Alan Blinder, Princeton University economist, and Mark Zandi, chief economist at Moody's Analytics, justify the federal government's massive spending response to the Great Recession in "How the Great Recession Was brought to an End," July 27, 2010. They use Moody's Analytics' U.S. economic model to simulate what would happen to economic indicators such as GDP, unemployment and consumer price index with and without federal government implementation of its fiscal stimuli and financial market policies. The authors listed the costly initiatives undertaken by Congress, the Federal Reserve and the last two White House administrations. At mid-2010, the cost was $1.59 trillion of which the American Recovery and Reinvestment Act of 2009 comprised $784 billion or nearly 50% of the total. If the methodology behind their economic modeling is viable, then it shows how badly the economy would have behaved if there were no fiscal stimuli and no policy response at all.

Zandi and Blinder write, "In this paper, we use the Moody's Analytics model of the U.S. economy—adjusted to accommodate some recent financial-market policies—to simulate the macroeconomic effects of the government's total policy response. We find that its effects on real GDP, jobs, and inflation are huge, and probably averted what could have been called Great Depression 2.0." The authors calculated that 2010 GDP, instead of the official 14,582,400, would have been 12,905,400, 8.5 million fewer people would have been working and price and wage deflation would have replaced inflation.

The authors' emphasis on how large the differences are is encompassed in this statement, "Remember, this is with no policy response at all. With outright deflation in prices and wages in 2009-2011, this dark scenario constitutes a 1930s-like depression."[164]

Figure 4-2 showing real GDP growth rate rising from 4th quarter 2008 to 4th quarter 2009 must have been comforting to federal authorities. What's troubling here is the generally underwhelming real GDP growth rate for 2010 through 2013 as shown in the same figure. Unfortunately the authors don't address other issues that may happen farther in the future as a result of the federal government's ongoing and future intervention actions.

All of this government spending is diverting money away from the more productive endeavors of the private sector. Harvard economics professor Robert Barro's research on this issue is outlined in his February 23, 2010 online Wall Street article, "The Stimulus Evidence One Year On." He stated that, "Over five years, my research shows an extra $600 billion of public spending at the cost of $900 billion in private expenditure. That's a bad deal."

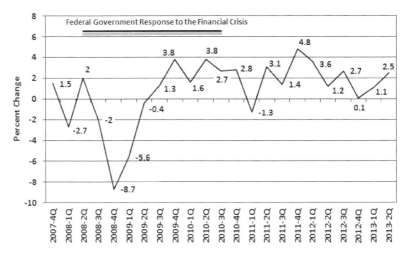

Figure 4-2: Real Gross Domestic Product, Percent Change from Preceding Quarter, Seasonally adjusted at annual rates
Courtesy: U.S. Department of Commerce, Bureau of Economic Analysis

Barro concludes, "The fiscal stimulus package of 2009 was a mistake. It follows that an additional stimulus package in 2010 would be another mistake." For the moment let's assume Barro and his fellow travelers are correct. Then our country may follow the Japan-like "lost decades" scenario. The federal government could have numerous cycles of stimulating, increasing GDP, falling back into low/no growth due to natural market forces and/or government debt reduction countermoves, then stimulating again.

The Fed Experiences Déjà vu

Central banks such as the Federal Reserve Bank, fearing deflation above all else, have and will use extraordinary measures to fight it. During the Great Recession and its aftermath, the Federal Reserve Bank under Chairman Ben Bernanke increased its balance sheet by over $2 trillion by purchasing toxic assets, providing liquidity to frozen markets, lending to troubled banks, implementing quantitative easing programs to buy U.S. Treasury bonds and buying other federal agencies' debt. Bernanke foretold of these policy actions in a November 2002 speech, "Deflation: Making Sure 'It' Doesn't Happen Here," made before the National

Economists Club when he was a member of the Board of Governors of the Federal Reserve System.[165]

In that 2002 speech, Bernanke spoke about lowering short term rates, one of the primary tools in the Fed's arsenal, "Because central banks conventionally conduct monetary policy by manipulating the short-term nominal interest rate, some observers have concluded that when that key rate stands at or near zero, the central bank has 'run out of ammunition'--that is, it no longer has the power to expand aggregate demand and hence economic activity."[166] The Fed funds rate has now been kept below 0.25% since January 2009 resulting in only slow economic growth and high unemployment in 2011.

Bernanke, in his speech, stated, "A more direct method, which I personally prefer, would be for the Fed to begin announcing explicit ceilings for yields on longer-maturity Treasury debt (say, bonds maturing within the next two years). The Fed could enforce these interest-rate ceilings by committing to make unlimited purchases of securities up to two years from maturity at prices consistent with the targeted yields. If this program were successful, not only would yields on medium-term Treasury securities fall, but (because of links operating through expectations of future interest rates) yields on longer-term public and private debt (such as mortgages) would likely fall as well."[167]

Nine years later on October 5, 2011, Bernanke, following the speech's script, announced "Operation Twist." The Fed will sell $400 billion of short-term Treasuries of three years remaining maturity or less and buy an equal amount of long-term Treasuries of six to thirty years remaining maturity. They will maintain the Fed funds rates at or below 0.25%. The Fed's intent is to lower mortgage and other lending rates to entice borrowers thus stimulating economic activity.[168] Commentators worry that the private sector may not respond and will continue to save, deleverage and avoid more indebtedness. In addition, the Fed may purchase a significant portion of Treasuries from foreign governments, financial institutions and foreign companies and citizens who would receive the cash rather than U.S. participants, thus creating fewer stimuli than calculated.

POSSIBLE MACROECONOMIC SCENARIOS

We believe the economic scenarios listed below are the most relevant.

> *Macroeconomic Scenario 1:* A V-shaped recovery similar to recoveries after average U.S. recessions prior to the Great Recession
>
> *Macroeconomic Scenario 2:* A long U-shaped recovery similar to Japan's low growth, high unemployment, "Lost Decades"
>
> *Macroeconomic Scenario 3:* A recession similar to the mild recessions of 1980, 1990-1991 and 2001
>
> *Macroeconomic Scenario 4:* A depression with 10% or more real GDP decline or a recession lasting 3 or more years
>
> *Macroeconomic Scenario 5:* Hyperinflationary money printing similar to the 1920s Weimar Republic hyperinflation

MACROECONOMIC SCENARIO 1: THE V-SHAPED RECOVERY THAT DIDN'T HAPPEN

A V-shaped recovery would entail a bottoming of economic indicators and then a quick improvement in many economic indicators such as employment, manufacturing, consumption and GDP. In Figure 4-1, the dashed line represents an example of a V-shaped recovery, but its configuration and any of the others should not be construed as an exact prediction of the future but as more of an average or approximation. The figure's V-shaped recovery curve incorporates economist David Rosenberg's calculation showing that two years after average U.S. recessions start, the percent annual growth rate of real GDP, quarter over quarter, rises to 7.5%. Some economists believe that the V-shaped recovery will eventually return to an average real GDP growth rate between 3% and 3.5%. This may have been true in the past, but the following table challenges this belief. The table shows that average real GDP growth rate has been steadily decreasing over the decades and is now well below the improperly perceived average rate of 3% to 3.5%.

At the Great Recession's two year mark, the nominal GDP growth rate was +1.1% and real (inflation-adjusted) GDP growth rate was -

1.5% from pre-recession peaks.[169] This large difference as compared to Rosenberg's 7.5% GDP growth rate estimate of average recessions is a stark reminder that the recovery is much slower than normal.

Table 4-1: Time Period vs. Average U.S. Real GDP, % Annual Rate, Quarterly

Time Period	Average U.S. Real Gross Domestic Product, Percent Annual Rate, Change from Preceding Quarter
1950 – 2009	3.22
1960 – 2009	3.16
1970 – 2009	2.89
1980 – 2009	2.79
1990 – 2009	2.56
2000 – 2009	1.63

Source: Bureau of Economic Analysis

Three "new normals" prevented a V-shaped recovery.

1. Unprecedented, massive levels of debt
2. Continuing deleveraging (that is, the paying off, defaulting on or restructuring of debt)
3. Long-term, high levels of unemployment

Debt

During the depths of the Great Recession, the percent ratio of debt to GDP (gross domestic product) of the total U.S. private, business and government sectors was a record 375%. The previous high was 300% just after World War II. The percent ratio of total debt to GDP is important as a measure of each sector's ability to service or pay off their debt. When GDP decreases and/or debt increases, the struggle to deleverage increases. An increasing number of economists such as David Rosenberg, Nouriel Roubini and Paul Krugman believe that, for a long time, perhaps for years, GDP growth will be 1% or 2% or <u>less</u>. This slow economic growth will lengthen the deleveraging and recovery process.

Another way to examine the economic effect of growing debt is to study how much U.S. GDP is increased by the increase in total annual U.S. debt. In Figure 4-3, we divide the annual change in GDP by the annual change in total U.S. debt expressed as ΔGDP/ΔDebt. It shows how one dollar of additional debt changes GDP. The Federal Reserve's z1 Flow of Funds Accounts of the United States provides data on the total U.S. debt under the Total Credit Market Debt tables for the private, business and government sectors. The graph clearly shows the declining efficiency of U.S. debt's ability to stimulate GDP growth since the 1950s. The total credit market debt increased 50x from 1964 until income could no longer support such towering debt and an increasing portion of that income had to be used for paying interest. When the economy could no longer support the growing debt, the Great Recession struck, which started in December 2007. The GDP downturn caused the sharp 2008-2010 dip in the ΔGDP/ΔDebt ratio.

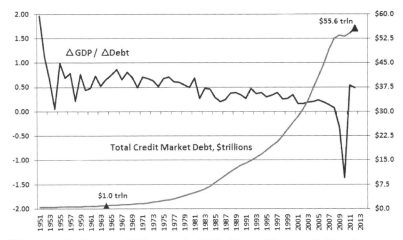

Figure 4-3: Ratio of Change in U.S. Gross Domestic Product over Change in U.S. Total Credit Market Debt versus Total Credit Market Debt, $trillions
Source: Federal Reserve Bank of St. Louis,
http://research.stlouisfed.org/fred2, Board of Governors of the Federal Reserve System, Flow of Funds Accounts of the United States z1, Table L.1 Credit Market Debt Outstanding

The 2010 ΔGDP/ΔDebt ratio was a record low at -1.49. 2010's ΔGDP was nearly the same as 2011's ΔGDP, but 2010's ΔDebt was -$394 billion, a large contraction, and 2011's ΔDebt increased by $844 billion. Thus it was this large increase in ΔDebt that caused the ratio's reversal to 0.67 in 2011. However this is likely not signaling that the ratio is now on a long term upward trend wherein the addition of U.S. debt will begin increasing our GDP by leaps and bounds.

So who was responsible for this debt? Figure 4-4 shows Federal government and government sponsored enterprises such as Fannie Mae and Freddie Mac adding trillions of dollars in U.S. debt from 2007 to 2011. The latter GSEs' purpose, along with other GSEs, was to bring home ownership to as many American citizens as possible by buying and guaranteeing mortgages and exchanging mortgage-backed securities (MBSs) for mortgage lenders' mortgage pools in the secondary mortgage market. During the period from 2007 to 2011, the federal government and the GSEs more than offset the small additions to debt or the hefty deleveraging by other sectors of society. The federal government's budget projections indicate more trillions in debt for many years. Japan's two lost decades of financial stimuli, continuing deficits, money printing, slow economic growth and towering debt is a cautionary tale for the United States.

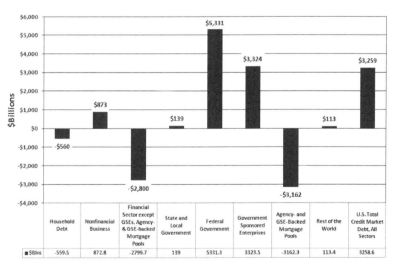

Figure 4-4: Increase or Decrease in U.S. Sector Total Credit Market Debt from 2007 to 2011, $billions
Source: Board of Governors of the Federal Reserve System, Flow of Funds Accounts of the United States z1, Table L.1 Credit Market Debt Outstanding

Deleveraging

In Chapter Three, we addressed the massive amounts of debt that the household and corporate sectors in the U.S. economy incurred. Although the nonfinancial business sector has added some debt over the last five years, both the household and financial business sectors, disciplined by the recession's punishing financial realities, have been deleveraging.

Throughout the boom times, hedge funds, banks, investment banks and individuals were leveraging money. For instance, financial institutions would borrow money short term anywhere in the world such as Japan or the United States at near zero rates and then invest or lend the funds longer term for higher rates of return. They would use many vehicles such as options, futures contracts or derivatives to leverage or multiply the effect of their available money. The payoff could be enormous or catastrophic. Paul McCulley, managing director of PIMCO, coined the term "shadow banking system" in August 2007 in Jackson Hole, Wyoming at the Federal Reserve's annual symposium. Shadow banks are usually intermediaries between investors and borrowers, do not take deposits and are therefore not subject to banking regulations.[170] The shadow banks created a massive amount of credit [debt] during the early 2000s decade, which shrank considerably during the last financial crisis. Deleveraging will be a painfully slow process.

Unemployment

The result of credit contraction, asset price deflation and deleveraging is increased unemployment. Future job prospects are bleak especially for the long term unemployed. Mortgage payment defaults, home foreclosures, hiring freezes and decreased economic activity don't augur well for the economy. Unemployment and fear of job loss will cause decreased consumption and greater saving rates. The latter describes the paradox of saving, which involves consumers saving more and spending less, leading to less business revenue, then more layoffs, less consumption, then more saving.

Inflation

After most V-Shaped recessions, inflation rates and economic activity usually rise significantly because the Federal Reserve and the federal government stimulated the economy using such tactics as lowering interest rates, providing financial stimuli and increasing the money supply. However, a V-Shaped recovery didn't develop after the Great Recession, which prevented the expected higher inflation rates from appearing. Many economists and bloggers insisted that we were headed for a greater inflation rate because of growing federal government debt in the trillions of dollars and the Federal Reserve Bank purchasing U.S. Treasury bonds through its multiple quantitative easing (QE) programs. However, all these factors haven't resulted in significant money supply growth or increases in credit. This was due in part to the banks not lending at adequate levels and instead rebuilding their balance sheets. Also businesses and individuals continue to deleverage in order to decrease their debt load.

MACROECONOMIC SCENARIO 2: THE LONG U-SHAPED RECOVERY WITH SLOW GROWTH, HIGH UNEMPLOYMENT

In my informal internet survey, economists advocating a slow growth, U-shaped recession have estimates of GDP growth rates that average between 1% and 2%. One of them is Gary Shilling, publisher of Insight Newsletter, who believes the economy will experience 10 years of slow 2% average GDP growth and rising unemployment. The actual problem, he says, is a deleveraging process that won't be painless or quick.[171] The average U.S. federal government's gross debt to GDP ratio from 1960 to 2000 was 46%. The ratio didn't include WWII when the U.S. paid for the enormous cost of waging a global war and arming allies. In 1946 the ratio rose to a peak of 121%. Currently the U.S. gross debt to GDP ratio has moved past Rogoff's and Reinhart's 90% tipping point where the ratio is highly likely to increase as tax revenues decrease and the economy stagnates.

Will the U.S. Mimic Japan's "Lost Decades"?

One of economists' and journalists' favorite arguments for a slow growth, U-shaped recession is a comparison between the U.S.

economy and Japan's "lost decades" during the 1990s and 2000s. Figure 4-5 shows Japan's grinding decline. Its stock market index, the Nikkei 225, fell over 75%. Its real GDP growth rate (percent change from previous quarter) averaged 0.33%, not even close to America's 2.56% average during the same period.

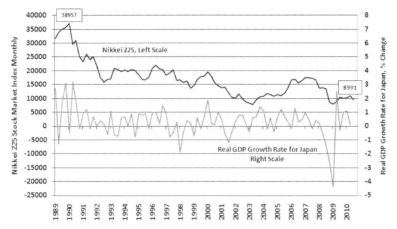

Figure 4-5: Nikkei 225 Stock Market Index Monthly and Real GDP Growth Rate for Japan, Percent Change from Previous Quarter
Courtesy: Yahoo Finance, Economic and Social Research Institute (ESRI), Cabinet Office - Government of Japan

Gary Shilling, author of the Insight newsletter, examined whether the U.S. economy could descend into a deflationary depression such as the one Japan has been experiencing for some twenty years or more. The similarities are of concern. Shilling notes that Standard & Poor's credit rating reduction of U.S. Treasuries from AAA to AA+ is similar to Japan's government bonds being downgraded in 1998 and S&P and Moody's downgrading them this year. The United States public debt to GDP ratio value is estimated at just above 73% as of December 2012 and is rising quickly. Shilling believes that the U.S. ratio will head to Japan's level of 125%. Both countries have dropped short-term interest rates to near zero, run deficits and implemented massive financial stimulus programs that resulted in only sluggish economic growth. Shilling reports that both central banks, finding themselves in "classic liquidity traps," resorted to quantitative easing which has had little effect. Dissimilarities are significant. Japan has financed its government debt internally unlike the U.S. which had to borrow much more from foreigners. The yen has been strong and relatively flat for two decades. Whenever the yen strengthens to Japanese exporters' detriment, their government will intervene in the currency markets to weaken the yen, but with only short term effect. The U.S., on the other hand, has been able to keep the dollar relatively weaker to our industry's advantage. Shilling concludes that U.S. advantages with respect to Japan are great and are unlikely to lead to a Japan-like deflationary depression.[172]

Richard C. Koo, chief economist for Nomura Research Institute and author of the book *Balance Sheet Recession*, presented a March 2009 paper titled "The Age of Balance Sheet Recessions: What Post-2008 U.S., Europe and China Can Learn from Japan 1990-2005." Koo's theory is that Japan experienced a balance sheet recession that was unlike the typical post-war recession. Japan's cumulative capital losses, which included stock market and land values, were a massive 1,500 trillion yen or an equivalent 45 trillion dollars from 1990 to the 2002 bottom.

The balance sheets of Japan's private sector were left with massive debt that they began dealing with by minimizing debt rather than maximizing profit. With Japan's private sector deleveraging, companies and households were and are saving and paying off debt. These monies enter the banks, but aren't lent out because of a dearth of qualified borrowers. Thus, as is happening in the United States, Japan's money velocity was decreasing as companies, banks and individuals spent less. Koo believes this contraction could continue until the private sector becomes too impoverished to save any money and Japan falls into depression.

The bad news for Japan is that their savings rate is falling as their population ages and begins retiring. When Japan's two lost decades began, the Japanese savings rate was 15% of GDP and is now 2 % in 2010.[173] This is the dreaded deflationary scenario that Koo believes can only be fixed when the private sector repairs its balance sheets.

Koo compares Japan's experience with those of the United States and shows the close parallels in the areas of residential and commercial real estate conditions, government bond yields, private sector deleveraging and the ineffectiveness of low interest monetary policy. Koo's conclusion is that government must provide massive fiscal stimuli to replace the lack of private sector demand.[174][175][176] Koo's solution is similar to Keynes' fiscal stimulus answer except that Koo sees the situation through the prism of his balance sheet recession ideas.

In 1990, the Japanese government debt to GDP ratio was 51%, a manageable number, but is now over 230%. As Japan runs out of their own citizens' savings to fund their growing government debts, will foreigners pick up the slack and buy Japan's government bonds?

What happens to Japan could happen to the U.S. and other countries troubled by high levels of sovereign debt. Japan's debt situation paints a bleak scenario and a warning for other nations. As we start 2013, Japan's government debt was nearing $14 trillion and its 10-year government bond interest rate was around 0.83%. Japan's Ministry of Finance estimates that 52% of Japan's 2012 tax revenues were used to service its debt. Quinn relates that if interest rates approach and then move past 3.5%, Japan will have to use all of its tax revenues to service its debt.[177]

The Atlantic Magazine's October 2012 article, "The Next Game," warns, "A crisis in Japan would most likely manifest as a collapse of confidence in the yen: At some point, Japanese citizens will decide that saving in any yen--denominated asset is not worth the risk. Then interest rates will rise; the capital position of banks, insurance companies, and pension funds will worsen (because they all hold long-maturing bonds, which fall in value when rates rise); and fears of insolvency will surface." If Japan, the world's third largest economy, defaulted on its government bonds or appreciably devalued its currency, then the shock would gravely affect other economies and markets. The article continues, "The most worrisome implication of Japan's increasingly precarious position, particularly in the wake of the 2008 crash and Europe's ongoing crisis, is that our financial systems appear to be returning to their inherently unstable nature, which plagued the 19th and early 20th centuries."[178]

Other economists believe that the U.S. may not follow Japan's slow growth because of demographics. Japan has a declining and an aging population. The numbers of Japanese aged 65 and older increased nearly twofold from 1990 to 2008. The elderly spend less and draw down their savings to meet living expenses as opposed to younger adults who form family units and consume more than senior citizens. Japan's population crested in 2004 at 127.8 million. Japan's Statistics Bureau in the Ministry of Health, Labour and Welfare estimates that their population will be 95.12 million in 2050.[179] The U.S., on the other hand, tends to balance its aging baby boomer population with much greater immigration.

As you can surmise from the above, the continuation of our Long U-shaped recovery scenario is not assured.

Stagflation

Stagflation occurs when an economy endures high inflation and high unemployment rates and low economic growth persists. An example of stagflation took place in the 1970s when all three stagflation conditions were met and inflation was especially elevated. As we have defined it, the economy isn't currently suffering from stagflation since deleveraging continues in the private sector causing consumer inflation to stay at levels below normal. Unemployment remains high and U.S. GDP growth rate remains lackluster. However, most people believe stagflation is gripping the nation. Even though the Consumer Price Index for all items is subdued, regular folks focus on inflation hotspots such as gasoline, grocery bills, college tuition and health care costs. Unlike the 1970s example, income is not keeping up with these rising costs as they did back then when wages did keep up with rising prices.

MACROECONOMIC SCENARIO 3: ARE WE DUE FOR ANOTHER RECESSION?

The recession clouds appear to be drawing closer. These well respected observers all see signs of economic weakness.

The Economic Cycle Research Institute studies economic cycles and forecasts recessions. Lakshman Achuthan and Anirvan Banerji, spokesmen for ECRI, explain that for the last 94 years, nearly three quarters of all recessions began while GDP was trending up. The start of a recession or the beginning of an economic contraction coincides with the top of the business cycle. Thus many economic indicators tend to be in an upswing initially. Also initial estimates for GDP growth rate and employment, which are often positive during the first stages of a recession, are frequently revised lower or into negative territory many months later. When making recession assessments, ECRI uses four important indicators, which are production, income, sales and employment. They say these economic indicators, if interpreted correctly, alert us about approaching recessions.[180]

In September 2011, ECRI wrote that a recession would likely begin either in the first quarter 2012 or in mid-2012, but that they wouldn't be able to ascertain if the latter were true until near the end of 2012. In a December 2012 announcement, ECRI's data showed that the recession started in July 2012 because production, income and sales data showed a peak in that month. Only the employment indicator has remained in an upslope for three months beyond July, which has happened in three of the last seven recessions. Many commentators have criticized ECRI because GDP and employment remain positive, although the 4th quarter 2012 GDP growth rate has dropped to -0.1%.[181]

Nouriel Roubini, NYU professor, sees five risks that might tip us into global recession. First, Europe's debt crisis and deepening recession is ongoing. Greece may still exit the Eurozone and the debt markets may spurn the governments of Italy and Spain. Second, the United States has not dealt with its fiscal, deficit and debt problems. Third, China's substandard growth has forced more stimuli whose effects will dwindle in the second half of the year. Fourth, growth of the other BRIC nations: Brazil, Russia and India are slowing. Fifth, Roubini warns that the entire Middle East is volatile and dangerous. He states that an Israeli/U.S. war with a nuclear-armed Iran is not likely, but if conflict became reality, then oil prices could surge by 20%. Roubini states, "While the chance of a perfect storm – with all of these risks materializing in their most virulent form – is low, any one of them alone would be enough to stall the global economy and tip it into recession. And while they may not all emerge in the most extreme way, each is or will be appearing in some form. As 2013 begins, the downside risks to the global economy are gathering force."[182]

Dr. John Hussman of Hussman Funds isn't that optimistic about prospects for a U.S. recession. In a December 31, 2012 Weekly Market Comment he wrote, "It strikes me that we have more hurdles for the financial markets beyond the fiscal cliff, including unresolved risks out of Europe, a likely but as yet unrecognized recession in the U.S., and continuing weakness in our return/risk estimate for the stock market, driven by a broad syndrome of overvalued, overbought, overbullish conditions."[183] In an earlier Comment, he opined that, "I continue to view the U.S. economy as being in a recession that began in the third quarter of this year."[184] Dr. Hussman compiles and calculates his own numerous indicators some of which are similar to those used by the Economic Cycle Research Institute.

The real (inflation-adjusted) GDP growth rate in Table 4-2 shows why many economists believed that the economy was on its way to recovery after mid-2009. The GDP growth rate rose to 4.0% in the 4th quarter 2009 most likely as the result of federal government bailouts and fiscal stimuli, which appears to have been temporary. In 2010 through 2011, GDP growth rates declined. The average for those two years was 2.18%. In past recessions, GDP growth rates a year after recession has ended usually have much more robust growth rates of 5% or higher.

Table 4-2: Real Gross Domestic Product, Percent Change from Preceding Quarter, Seasonally adjusted at annual rates

2009				2010				2011				2012				2013	
Q1	Q2	Q3	Q4	Q1	Q2	Q3	Q4	Q1	Q2	Q3	Q4	Q1	Q2	Q3	Q4	Q1	Q2
-5.3	-0.3	1.3	3.9	1.6	3.9	2.8	2.8	-1.3	3.2	1.4	4.9	3.7	1.2	2.8	0.1	1.1	2.5

Source: Department of Commerce, Bureau of Economic Analysis

We believe the keys to the timing for a recession are government intervention, the European sovereign debt crisis, unemployment, and the housing market. Government intervention will likely have the biggest effect.

A sufficiently large government intervention such as a Federal Reserve Bank quantitative Easing 3 (QE3) and/or European Community Bank Long Term Refinancing Operation (LTRO) program could throw a recession forecast out the window. However, market and economic forces may become so overwhelming that recession arrives sooner rather later. The federal government ended quantitative easing 2 in June 2011. The Fed is using this term instead of the negatively regarded "printing money" phrase. The Fed attempts, through quantitative easing, to inflate the money supply by boosting bank's excess reserves. The Federal

Reserve Bank, with a mouse click, creates money ex-nihilo or "out of nothing." That newly created money can be used to buy nearly any financial asset such as U.S. Treasury bonds, corporate bonds, mortgage-backed securities or even stocks in the same manner as the central bank of Japan buying Japanese ETFs or Israel's central bank buying U.S. stocks. The banks are supposed to use the fractional reserve banking system to expand the money supply and boost money velocity.[185] However, the banks will likely be cautious for the long term, thus not increasing the nation's money supply to any extent. A genuine private sector recovery will be postponed like the "can kicked down the road" due to private investment funds being taken out of the economy.

As you read this, a recession may already have started. It's become more obvious that the economy is slowing. The following additional organizations and individuals have announced recessionary warnings. In their October 2012 World Economic Outlook report, "Coping with High Debt and Sluggish Growth," the International Monetary Fund repeated their warning that the European sovereign debt crisis, an emerging market slowdown and continuing deleveraging could lead the world into a global recession. "...the fund says its modeling shows the risk of recession is "alarmingly high", with a 17 per cent chance that global growth will miss its forecasts and come in below 2 per cent, which would be consistent with a recession in advanced economies."[186] In November 2012, the Organization for Economic Cooperation and Development (OECD) warned, "The world economy is far from being out of the woods," OECD Secretary-General Angel Gurría said during the Economic Outlook launch in Paris. "The US 'fiscal cliff', if it materialises, could tip an already weak economy into recession, while failure to solve the euro area crisis could lead to a major financial shock and global downturn."[187] Economist David Rosenberg, in a September 2012 Breakfast with Dave newsletter, wrote that one indicator, a subcomponent of the Durable Goods report, the 3-month average of core capex orders (capital expenditure orders) is particularly prescient in predicting whether or not the economy is in recession. In August 2012, the latter gauge was down 4.1%. Rosenberg relates that when it has reached this value, past data shows that the nation has been in recession every time.[188]

Shortly after the Great Recession ended, many analysts warned that a double dip recession similar to the one in the early 1980s was a distinct possibility. The last double dip recession in 1981 started a year after the one in 1980. However, the National Bureau of Economic Research decided they were two separate recessions occurring close together. An internet search finds varying definitions for a double dip recession. We have now progressed at least three years since the last recession ended and won't know for up to a year if a recession has started.

Disinflation

Disinflation occurs when the inflation rate declines. Prices increase but more slowly than in previous periods. For an example of long duration disinflation, we refer you back to Figure 2-11: GDP versus 10 Year Govt Bond Yield versus Annual Inflation Rate, 1953 to 2012. The latter reveals that the annual percent change in the inflation rate topped around 1979 and has been declining ever since. Japan also experienced the same disinflationary period which started in 1974 and percent annual change in the inflation rate has been descending ever since. On a more granular scale, the United States has seen disinflation during many recessions since the Great Depression. We have had 30 years of U.S. disinflation starting in the 1980s. Recently the interest rate on the 10 year U.S. Treasury bond has dropped below 2%. This low an interest rate has not been seen since the 1930s and 1940s when the 10 year ranged from about 1.95% to 2.8%. It may indicate that bond interest rates are coming close to their lows and will eventually rise when the servicing of government debt is seen as increasingly difficult.

MACROECONOMIC SCENARIO 4: IS DEPRESSION POSSIBLE?

There isn't any universally recognized definition for what a depression is. Even the National Bureau of Economic Research (NBER), which many federal government agencies refer to for starting and ending dates of recessions, avoids defining depression. The NBER's online Frequently Asked Questions page contains the statement: "The NBER does not separately identify depressions."

The Economist magazine wrote that their internet search for a depression definition suggested two conditions, which were 1) a real GDP decline of 10% or more or 2) a recession persisting three years or more. In America, our Great Depression and the 1873 through 1879 depression lasting for five years plus five months both qualify.[189]

Gluskin Sheff economist David Rosenberg believes the United States is already in a depression. He says that we don't see signs reminiscent of a 1930s-style Great Depression for many reasons. Rosenberg cites the 46 million U.S. citizens on food stamps, which are in the form of debit cards, so that breadlines are nowhere in evidence. Government transfer payments now constitute 20% of all household income, which is larger than during President Lyndon Johnson's era of "The Great Society." As further evidence, Rosenberg mentioned his unemployment estimate of 14.8%, far higher than the rate given by the Bureau of Labor Statistics. In addition, from 2007 to 2010, median household net worth fell by 40%.[190]

In his book, *The New Depression: The Breakdown of the Paper Money Economy*, economist Richard Duncan argues that unprecedented credit growth led to unsustainable economic booms in the periods from 1914 to 1930 and 1971 to 2008. Both booms began when money's convertibility into gold eroded and eventually terminated. When lenders were unable to shoulder the debt that credit growth created, the 1930s Great Depression followed. Duncan describes how the latest boom could lead to a "New Great Depression."[191]

Duncan theorizes about two paths by which a "disaster scenario" could progress. A trigger could be derivatives, rogue trades, a sovereign debt default or more home price deterioration. In any case, quick and escalating losses would throw the banks into crisis. If financial backstops were late, total credit market debt (TCMD) could shrink by a third just as the money supply shrank by a third from 1929 to 1939. Because the dollar is no longer backed by gold, Duncan defines a credit instrument as a dollar with an obligation to pay interest. Thus Duncan defines credit as being nearly identical with money. Increasing credit in an economy has nearly the same effect as increasing the money supply. Credit destruction by a third would cause GDP to decline by a similar amount leading to severe depression.[192]

Duncan's second path, though slower, but also economically destructive, is protectionism. As the economy weakens, rising unemployment would cause workers to ask Congress for trade tariffs against other exporting countries. Prices would escalate causing inflation and interest rates to rise. Exporting countries would retaliate with their own tariffs and currency manipulation. World trade would contract severely, businesses would fail, unemployment would skyrocket, private investment would plunge and a systemic bank crisis would develop.[193] Duncan isn't forecasting that a depression is coming, but is stating under what circumstances it could happen.

Although the causes that might lead to a disaster scenario are numerous, we think that the manner in which government intervenes will be a primary factor in determining whether a depression happens or not.

In Chapter Three, the section titled "REDUCING THE DEBT LOAD WILL TAKE TIME" explained how it would take years to reduce indebtedness from their unparalleled levels. The private sector, that is individuals, households and businesses, has to curtail consumption for years to complete such an endeavor. The federal government has attempted to replace this missing demand/consumption to facilitate economic recovery. The spending from their bailouts, fiscal stimuli and the Fed's quantitative easing programs has been less and less effective in ramping up permanent economic growth and raising asset prices than forecast.

The federal government has gone deeply into debt to jumpstart the economy. But according to the Federal Reserve System, the nominal household net worth loss from 2007 year end to mid-2009 was $14 trillion. From the October 2007 peak to the March 2009 bottom, the market capitalization of the Dow Jones Wilshire 5000 index that includes almost all United States stocks dropped by $11 trillion. The U.S. housing market lost approximately $6.1 trillion from the 2006 peak through 2008.[194] These kinds of numbers are examples of just how big the market declines were relative to the federal government's resources. Real world markets and people's real world decisions may simply overwhelm whatever borrowed money that governments throw at our economic problems.

Global demographic trends are also working against a quick economic recovery. Bill Gross, managing director and co-CIO of PIMCO, Pacific Investment Management Company, proposed, "I will go so far as to say that not only growth but capitalism itself may be in part dependent on a growing population." In his August 2010 Investment Outlook report, Gross stated that, although observers note worldwide growth rates in population have been decreasing after 1970 without economic consequences until the Great Recession, nations needed to bolster their GDP growth rates using "artificial asset price stimulation" and copious credit growth to finance excessive personal consumption. Gross wrote that eventually as U.S. household debt escalated and personal consumption reached 70% of GDP, the economy rolled over.[195]

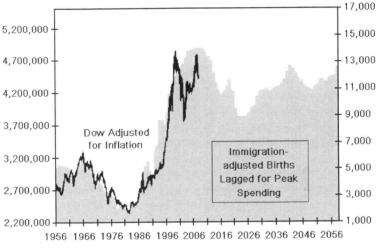

Figure 4-6: The Spending Wave
Courtesy: HS Dent Publishing

Economic forecaster Harry Dent argues in his 2008 book *The Great Depression Ahead* that demographics data points to the "next great depression." Dent contends that a generational spending peak in the U.S. and the Dow Jones Industrial Average's bear market are no mere coincidence. He graphs the immigration-adjusted birth cycle curve that peaked in 2009. Dent moved the birth cycle curve forward to the requisite 46-50 year age group (think baby boomers) that spends the most at that time during their life spans. When Dent overlaps the inflation-adjusted Dow Jones over the birth cycle, the two follow each other quite well from 1956 to the present. If

Dent's graph is a glimpse into the future, then his graph shows consumption declining until at least 2020 and the economy will likely follow along.[196] Dent shows that the same phenomena are happening on a global scale. In 1990, Japan was the first nation to grow old and crest population-wise and that is when their stock markets and GDP growth rates began declining. In 2010, Europe, Eastern Europe, Russia, the United States, Australia and New Zealand aged and peaked.[197]

Thus a demographically caused spending decline with associated massive debt, private sector deleveraging and business losses could generate continuing credit contraction and debt default, and lead to much greater economic trouble than many of us expect.

Deflation Prospects

As in Chapter One, we define deflation as a decrease in the supply of credit and money that, in turn, leads to a nominal price level lower than it would have been without the deflation. Debt levels are most likely having the most effect on deflation. A great deal of economic theory examines the relationship between debt and deflation. Because of the 2008 credit crunch and the Great Recession, two economists' theories have received renewed interest. Hyman Minsky's financial instability hypothesis and Irving Fisher's debt-deflation theory both came to many of the same conclusions. When income can no longer service debt levels that have become too great, prices begin to drop. The purchasing power of the currency increases causing debtors to struggle to pay off their debts in increasingly valuable money. The real, or inflation-adjusted, amount of debt increases. Debt deleveraging contributes to more deflation. Consumers and businesses begin delaying purchases because they believe prices will move lower in the future. This contributes to more price deflation. If government authorities do not intervene, Fisher believed this debt-deflation spiral could lead to depression.[198][199]

Both the Consumer Price Index (CPI) and the Finished Goods portion of the Producer Price Index, as measured in year over year percent changes, is warning us that deflationary times and recession may be approaching. As shown in the figure, during the Great Recession, the year-over-year percent changes did descend into deflation territory.

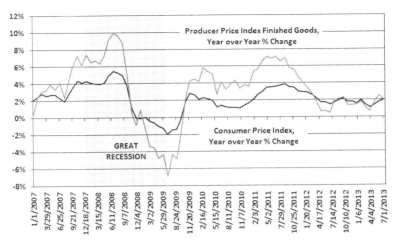

Figure 4-7: Consumer Price Index versus Producer Price Index Finished Goods, Year over Year Percent Change
Source: U.S. Bureau of Labor Statistics

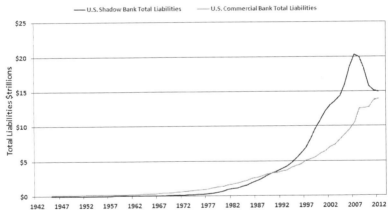

Figure 4-8: Shadow Bank Liabilities versus Commercial Bank Liabilities, $ trillions
Source: Flow of Funds Accounts of the United States, Federal Reserve Bank and Federal Reserve Bank of New York, 2012 is for the 1st quarter 2012[200]

Another key indicator of deflation at work is the decline of private sector credit. In 2011, United States total credit market debt was $54.1 trillion while the M2 money supply was $9.7 trillion. Figure 4-8 illustrates the decline since 2007 of approximately $6 trillion in shadow bank liabilities or credit while commercial bank liabilities increased $3.5 trillion in the same period. The data in this graph illustrate the large forces at work in the economy. This 2 to 1 disparity of shadow bank liabilities (credit) decrease over commercial bank liabilities increase is the reason why overall credit inflation or price inflation has been muted. If shadow bank liabilities cross below commercial bank liabilities and continue to do so, then price deflation could appear quickly. The shadow bank liabilities are total GSE liabilities and GSE pool securities, open market paper, net securities loaned, total liabilities of ABS issuers, total repurchase agreements liabilities and total shares outstanding of money market mutual funds. Of these, ABS or asset backed securities liabilities has declined the most, some $2.57 trillion. This is not surprising since the underlying assets were portfolios of loans on assets such as residential and commercial real estate, autos or boats. The money market mutual funds were next in deleveraging with a $1.22 trillion decline. The declines in repurchase agreements liabilities, GSE liabilities and GSE pool securities, open market paper and net securities loaned were $0.97 trillion, $0.72 trillion, $0.97 trillion and $0.59 trillion respectively.

Economist John Mauldin, president of Millennium Wave Advisors, writes in his and coauthor Jonathan Tepper's book, *Endgame: The End of the Debt Supercycle and How It Changes Everything*, "Where do we stand on the issue of deflation versus inflation? We think we'll have both. Deflation first, and then inflation. It will probably take further downturns and a greater collapse of borrowing and lending to induce even more extreme responses from governments. In the endgame, we see a very low likelihood that the Federal Reserve and other central banks will be able to do the right thing and get us out of the deflationary problems we face without letting inflation get out of hand or causing large collateral damage."[201] Mauldin writes about the causes of deflation such as the forces attempting to contract the money supply and how money velocity has been shrinking since mid-2006. He foresees the endgame or the end of the Debt Supercycle.

In a 2002 speech "Deflation: Making Sure 'It' Doesn't Happen Here," then Federal Reserve Board Governor Ben Bernanke explained how the Fed would fight deflation. His comments were a clear roadmap of decisions he has made so far in his tenure as Fed Chairman. He has used the Fed's money "printing press" liberally, injected liquidity into the financial system and dropped the Fed funds rate close to zero percent. One tactic the Fed cannot implement because the dollar is the world's reserve currency is depreciation, which other countries put into practice by setting a new fixed rate with respect to the dollar. To gain the same effect, Bernanke described how the Federal Reserve could purchase large quantities of other countries' currencies.[202][203] The Fed would be flooding the world with dollars. In retaliation other nations could engage in currency wars thus blunting the Federal Reserve's actions.

MACROECONOMIC SCENARIO 5: COULD HYPERINFLATIONARY MONEY PRINTING HAPPEN?

The 1920s Weimar Republic hyperinflation is one of the most famous and certainly one of the most well documented. Starting from 1918, the value of paper Marks depreciated until one trillion were required to equal one gold Mark in 1923. In 1914, Germany severed the link between gold and the Mark to finance the costs of waging World War I. Unlike today's electronic debt monetization, Germany ran actual paper printing presses, sometimes night and day, to fund war costs, to pay workers and to buy foreign currencies. Under the Treaty of Versailles, the Reparations Commission required Germany to pay war reparations in foreign currency, gold Marks, hard assets or goods rather than paper Marks.[204] Although Germany's industrial base was untouched by World War I, the Weimar Republic hyperinflation left Germany's social order in chaos and its economy in tatters. Pensioners and fixed income recipients were left destitute, savings were wiped out and lenders and insurance companies bankrupted. Today decades later, Germany's national memory of that hyperinflation shapes their actions and decisions in dealing with the European sovereign debt crisis. They dread inflation and understand that hyperinflating a country's money supply simply transfers the problem from the government onto the backs of the people.[205]

Many observers believe the United States will experience hyperinflation similar to the Weimar Republic's when the economy begins to recover and the liquidity that Congress and the Federal Reserve Bank provided during and after the Great Recession causes money velocity to accelerate.

We believe this is unlikely for a number of reasons.

In Chapter One, we described how the central banks, such as the Federal Reserve Bank, can create money ex nihilo (out of nothing) by electronically crediting their own accounts. The Fed then purchases assets such as bonds, securities or other assets in open market operations from banks, financial institutions and companies. The banking system increases the money supply by lending money not only from deposited funds but also by borrowing the money to meet the reserve ratio requirement or lending money gained from selling toxic assets to the Fed. Thus our money is monetized debt. Hyperinflationists believe that, when the economy finally starts to recover, the banks will lower lending standards, the private sector will ramp up loan demand and prodigious amounts of money will flow out of the banks and into the economy. At the present time, the banks aren't lending at the levels required for that to happen. Private loan demand is still low and could be for years while deleveraging continues. In Chapter Three, we wrote about author Richard Duncan's theory that credit growth spurred the boom times from the 1960s to 2007. In 2011, U.S. credit was $54.1 trillion nearly 6 times larger than M2 money supply at $9.2 trillion. Thus the Federal Reserve's efforts to hyperinflate would be far more dependent on creating credit growth in the private sector than increasing the nation's money supply.

Suppose you're living on fixed income. An interest check from your General Motors corporate bond arrives in your mail box. You run down to your local Starbucks to get your weekly decaf latte before its purchasing power drops even further. That check used to defray a big portion of your grocery bill, but hyperinflation robbed it of its purchasing power. Can you sell your GM bonds? Yes, but the money you get has much less purchasing power than when you originally bought it. And you're not alone. Most corporations, government entities and individuals are in the same boat. Those with bonds, savings, pensions and cash would not do well. The social unrest and protests could morph into riots and revolution.

Let's assume that when hyperinflation starts, the dollar is still the reserve currency for the global economy. Thus commodities and other assets such as oil are priced in dollars. It means that prices worldwide would rise as prices in the United States climb. The international protest would be swift and angry. We believe that foreign governments would support the dollar only if the United

States acted swiftly to stop hyperinflation. Otherwise those same countries, corporations and individuals would sell their holdings of U.S. Treasury bonds. U.S. Treasury bond interest rates could rise precipitously and cause Treasury bond auctions to fail making the borrowing of money to fund U.S. federal government deficits very difficult. Other countries would continue to vie for reserve currency status. All the economic advantages that accrue to the United States having reserve currency status would end.

The political heat on Congress and the Federal Reserve Bank would be intense. They understand how terrible social and economic conditions could get and won't stand by idly while hyperinflation escalates. According to the Federal Reserve, excess reserves of depositary institutions have risen to over a trillion dollars since the 2008 credit crunch. These are the reserves that would help provide the fuel for hyperinflation. The Fed believes they can drain a sufficient amount of these reserves from the banks when necessary.

In response to hyperinflation, the Federal Reserve Bank could launch the Volcker solution. Volcker was Federal Reserve Chairman from 1979 to 1987. During his term, inflation crested at 13.5% in 1981. Volcker increased the Fed funds rate from 1979's 11.2% to 1981's 20%. Inflation dropped to 3.2% in 1983.[206] Today, the Fed could raise the discount interest rate or Fed funds rate. In 2012, the Federal Reserve started the Term Deposit Facility. Participating banks depositing into this facility receive interest and decrease the banks' reserves. The Federal Reserve Bank has and could use reverse repurchase agreements or RRPs to borrow money from primary dealers, which also shrinks banks' reserves. Primary dealers are pre-approved banks that purchase U.S. Treasury bonds at auction and redistribute them to their clients. [207][208]

KCM Investment Advisors, in their January 2013 Quarterly Commentary, reported on the burgeoning balance sheets of the six largest central banks. The Federal Reserve's total assets were nearly $3 trillion and all six have a total over $15 trillion. Their clear intent is to continue to increase money supplies thus thwarting a possible recession and deflation. If their program works, then inflation will persist and prices of assets such as homes and stocks will keep rising. KCM concluded from their studies of past periods having "low and rising inflation" that equities and commodities do well and certain fixed income investments do not. They warn that the central banks' "money printing" could spawn an "inflationary hurricane," which they believe won't happen in 2013. However they make no mention of inflation tendencies in later years.[209]

Figure 4-9: The Biggest Six Central Bank Balance Sheets (\$trlns) (U.S., U.K., ECB, Japan, China, and Switzerland)
Source: Blanco Research, PIMCO and KCM Investment Advisors

STEPS TO ECONOMIC RECOVERY AND PROSPERITY

Forecasting macroeconomic scenarios is complicated by many factors. In this chapter's previous section, "The Role of Government Intervention," we explained Ray Dalio's concepts of countries' ugly deflationary deleveraging, beautiful deleveraging, and ugly inflationary deleveraging and how these results are determined by the quantity and speed of "1) austerity, 2) debt reduction, 3) transferring wealth from the haves to the have-nots and 4) debt monetization." Dalio believes that if countries properly orchestrate and implement the correct level of these four processes, then economic recovery and renewed growth can be achieved.

1. Austerity: The advanced economies must follow appropriate levels of austerity to begin a recovery that sustains renewed economic growth. Too much austerity cuts economic growth, lowers income and revenue and delays recovery. Too little austerity impedes debt reduction.

In *The Endgame: The End of the Debt Supercycle and How It Changes Everything*, John Mauldin and Jonathan Tepper wrote, "Essentially, the debt supercycle is the decades 'long growth of debt from small and manageable levels, to a point where bond markets rebel and the debt has to be restructured or reduced. A program of austerity must be undertaken to bring the debt back to acceptable levels."[210]

The McKinsey Global Institute, in their July 2011 report, "Debt and deleveraging: The global credit bubble and its economic consequences," studied 45 instances of national deleveraging starting with the 1930s depression. Of the 45, financial crisis preceded deleveraging or a significant reduction of the debt to GDP ratio in 32 of the occurrences. The McKinsey Global Institute concluded that austerity was the most common deleveraging method for the advanced economies. McKinsey reported that reducing debt through inflation, massive defaults and growing your economy were comparatively uncommon.[211]

2. Debt Reduction: Dalio emphasizes the need to reduce the debt-to-GDP ratio which allows debt servicing to become manageable. Both the government and private sector can't cut debt too rapidly because too much debt default and restructuring is counterproductive. Rapid debt reduction could hasten the decline of associated markets such as housing and reinforce what Dalio calls a "self-reinforcing downward spiral" in which declining confidence adversely affects markets and delays economic recovery.[212]

3. Wealth transfer: Dalio notes that countries can attempt debt reduction through transference of wealth from the haves to the have-nots. The methods might be taxes on the affluent or "rich" European nations bailing out indebted peripheral European countries. However, he warns that they seldom provide deleveraging relief in any significant amounts.[213]

4. Debt monetization: Countries that have reserve currency status such as the United States can monetize the debt or "print paper money" and financially stimulate to fight deflation. However, if carried on for too long or at excessive levels, the process can ultimately cause Dalio's "ugly inflationary deleveraging."

Dalio cites the U.S. from 1933 to 1937 as a time when the U.S. engaged in a "beautiful deleveraging," balancing just the right amounts of money "printing" and devaluation of the dollar against gold to counteract deflationary forces of austerity and debt reduction.[214]

The following are some additional helpful steps toward recovery:

5. Reduce government deficits, allow deleveraging to continue and permit markets to clear

We and many other analysts and economists have argued that the large amounts of global debt are unsustainable. Authorities must allow debt to sink to levels that income can sustain so that economic growth can resume. Among the nations deleveraging, the United States is likely doing a much better job than many others. McKinsey Global Institute believes U.S. households may have completed one half the necessary deleveraging and will have completed it by mid-2013. McKinsey opines, "These examples illustrate that an economy is ready to resume sustained growth after private-sector deleveraging when certain conditions are in place: the financial sector is stabilized and lending volumes are rising; structural reforms are in place to boost productivity and enable GDP growth; credible medium-term public deficit reduction plans have been adopted and restore confidence; exports are growing; private investment resumes; and the housing market is stabilized and residential construction is reviving."[215]

6. Reform Social Security, Medicare and Medicaid

Stanford University economist John Taylor opines, "Right now, the entitlement spending is expected to grow way beyond something that anybody expects to be realistic. We just have to contain that growth. In other words, keep the spending from growing even further as a share to GDP. We do that in a way where we use the markets, the rule of law and incentives, it will be a better system. Some proposals out there to reform Medicare, Medicaid and keep spending down will lead to better health care. That is what we should be striving to do."[216]

7. Achieve greater energy independence, efficiency, and sustainability

As a nation consuming huge quantities of fossil fuels, we are exposed to the whims of untrustworthy foreign governments, the high probability of global warming and other harmful environmental effects. Separating the best energy policies from the emotional appeals and junk science is difficult for most of us who might be time-deprived. To help clear the air, we recommend a free book "*Sustainable Energy — without the hot air*" written by physics professor David MacKay at the University of Cambridge. His book is technical due to the subject's nature, but is well written and understandable. Although the book is United Kingdom centered, many of the arguments and facts can also apply to the United States. For instance, MacKay includes an informative Chapter 31 titled "Energy Plans for Europe, America, and the World" in which you'll learn that the average American uses twice as much energy per day as an average European or Japanese.[217]

The U.S. Energy Information Administration says we are already starting to become more energy independent and efficient due to new technologies, discoveries of new oil and natural gas deposits, recovery from old fields and development of solar and wind energy. They estimate the U.S. will become increasingly energy independent and decrease energy imports over the next thirty years. Energy imports that comprised 27% of all energy expended in 2007 could drop to 9% in 2040.[218]

8. Improve Productivity and Competitiveness

Improving the nation's labor productivity will also boost its global competitiveness and enhance economic growth. We must reverse the last three decades' decreasing U.S. GDP growth rates and the shrinking number of working U.S. citizens as a percent of total U.S. population. The McKinsey Global Institute in a February 2011 report, "Growth and renewal in the United States: Retooling America's economic engine," believes that productivity will be gained through "efficiency gains, innovation, and increasing the value and quality of goods and services produced." They propose seven priorities the United States should tackle to promote productivity gains that will drive economic expansion.[219]

9. Build, repair and replace infrastructure

Table 4-3: American Infrastructure Report Card

Infrastructure	Grade
Aviation	D
Bridges	C
Dams	D
Drinking Water	D-
Energy	D+
Hazardous Waste	D
Inland Waterways	D-
Levees	D-
Public Parks & Recreation	C-
Rail	C-
Roads	D-
Schools	D
Solid Waste	C+
Transit	D
Wastewater	D-
America's Infrastructure GPA:	D

We have before us a great opportunity to improve our lives, spur economic growth and put people back to work. Most of us are aware of the nation's crumbling infrastructure, but rarely give it much thought until systems fail us. We know that infrastructure greases the wheels of economic growth and business. Fail to address infrastructure problems and the infrastructure will fail us. Programs to repair, replace or augment American infrastructure must be sustained over long periods without interruption.

Be sure to access the sobering American Society of Civil Engineers' "Report Card for America's Infrastructure" at http://www.infrastructurereportcard.org and review ASCE solutions at http://www.infrastructurereportcard.org/solutions.

The American Society of Civil Engineers estimates the United States must spend $2.2 trillion over the next five years to improve its infrastructure from grade D to B.[220]

10. Improve the small business and entrepreneurial environment

Most of the jobs in our economy are provided by small business rather than the big corporations. According to the U.S. Census Bureau, 99.7% of the nearly 27 million businesses in the United States are small businesses. Here are some suggestions that could help small businesses and their ability to create employment.

- Reduce the regulatory burden on small business and the amount of regulatory paperwork.
- Reform big business legislation that hampers and is often not applicable to small business.
- Pass permanent tax cuts and tax credits preferably having no sunset clause. United States corporations pay at higher tax rates than any other country except Japan.
- Help small businesses obtain greater access to credit.
- Provide educational assistance to small business owners and entrepreneurs.[221][222]

11. Improve education and educational institutions

A prime example of innovative ideas in education is the Khan Academy founded by Salman Khan who initially created and posted online thousands of free educational videos on math, science, economics and social science subjects. In support, Microsoft's Bill Gates and others have provided millions of dollars to the Academy. In classic education, teachers aim their instruction to the middle proficiency of their class. However in many cases, bright learners become bored and the laggard pupils struggle and drop behind. In those classrooms where teachers have adopted Khan Academy videos, each student learns at their own pace. Teachers can quickly help struggling students. Other classmates leap far ahead of their grade levels. Detractors mainly in the education ranks, claim, amongst other criticisms, that Khan's methods lead to rote memorization and less teacher-student interaction. Visit Kahn Academy at http://www.khanacademy.org/[223]

The highest priority in educational reform is likely improving teacher quality and teacher effectiveness. Craig Barrett is one of the founders of *Change the Equation*, a non-profit organization for the improvement of education in science, technology, engineering, and math. Barrett wants the education system to enlist teachers from the top of their college graduating classes, turn experts into teachers and have students study the material they will teach. Steven Brill, also of *Change the Equation* and author of *Class Warfare: Inside the Fight to Fix America's Schools*, wants teachers' union contracts to emphasize performance instead of security and seniority.[224]

CHAPTER FIVE

Macroeconomic Scenario and Risk Factor Analysis

"Don't put all your eggs in one economic basket."

Figure 5-1
Source: Betty Matsumoto-Schuch

INTRODUCTION

The first four chapters of this book described and analyzed the historical events and possible causes leading up to the Great Recession of 2007-2009. We identified those economic analysts who correctly foresaw the coming of that crisis and passed on what lessons could be learned from them. In the last chapter, we draw upon the resources of those economic analysts and other relevant organizations to provide five different macroeconomic scenarios that could unfold over the next several years. First, readers will learn how macroeconomic events affect their portfolios. Second, elements of a broad-based, investing framework will be explained. Third, we explain how to incorporate the different macroeconomic scenarios into this framework.

FRAMEWORK FOR INVESTING

Adhering to the disciplines of building your personal framework for investing provides guidance, a systematic approach and greater clarity during the investment decision making process. Although Modern Portfolio Theory (MPT) has been criticized, especially during these volatile market periods, MPT can still provide a starting point. We believe many of the fundamental principles, while often forgotten, are still valid. When properly diversified, MPT based portfolios contain asset class exposures for most conceivable macroeconomic scenarios. An important MPT principle is that holding asset classes that move in different directions during a crisis reduces volatility, a key benefit of diversification. As an example, one of the most common asset flows is from equities to bonds during a risk-off period and from bonds to equities during a risk-on climate.

Modern Portfolio Theory (MPT) Defined

"The fundamental concept behind MPT is that the assets in an investment portfolio should not be selected individually, each on their own merits. Rather, it is important to consider how each asset changes in price relative to how every other asset in the portfolio changes in price.

"Investing is a tradeoff between risk and expected return. In general, assets with higher expected returns are riskier. For a given amount of risk, MPT describes how to select a portfolio with the highest possible expected return. Or, for a given expected return, MPT explains how to select a portfolio with the lowest possible risk (the targeted expected return cannot be more than the highest-returning available security, of course, unless negative holdings of assets are possible. "[225]

Thus, the intent of MPT principles is to diversify one's portfolio and add greater safety and value. Based on key quantitative definitions of risk and return, MPT provides a starting point for building and maintaining a diversified portfolio.

Core MPT principles to understand are: asset allocation, correlations, diversification, standard deviation, and risk. The most important one to grasp is correlation. To reduce risk in a portfolio, asset classes must not correlate, that is, fluctuate in a similar fashion. A simple definition of correlation is:

> "In investments, correlation describes how closely related the price movement of different securities or asset classes is. The higher the correlation, the more closely prices move in the same direction and by similar amounts."[226]

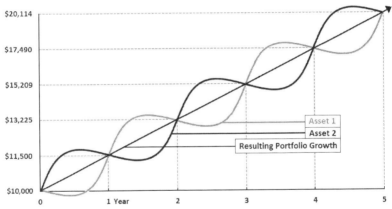

Figure 5-2: Hypothetical No-Risk Portfolio, Growth of $10,000
Source: http://www.investorsolutions.com/news/129/121/Adding-International-Equities-to-Your-Portfolio/

The way to minimize risk or volatility is to have various components of the portfolio negatively correlate or have low correlations to each other. Figure 5-2 depicts a purely hypothetical portfolio with two asset classes that illustrates this point in a simple and effective manner. The investor's goal is to identify complementary asset classes that provide a "diversifying benefit" to each other and also satisfy the long-term, expected return requirements of the investor. Original MPT work was focused on analyzing the correlations between stocks and bonds and ultimately finding the optimal portfolio for any given level of risk or return. This process is still called mean variance optimization or MVO.

MPT and Economics

Less spoken about when discussing MPT are implicit economic assumptions: an investor doesn't need to know (and perhaps doesn't want to know) anything about where the economy and/or financial markets are heading. The belief is that with a sufficient time horizon, cycles in the economy will come and go, and appropriately diversified portfolios will perform as the markets will, following the Efficient Market Theory. Most buy and hold investors would argue that markets go up over the long term and a properly diversified portfolio will generate reasonable "market type returns" commensurate with targeted return and risk goals.

Post MPT

Following the Nobel Prize winning work of Harry Markowitz and others, there were critics who pointed to some shortcomings of MPT and came to be known as post-MPT proponents. Objections were varied. Some pointed to the weakness of some of the MPT assumptions. For example, they argued that investors are not "rational." Some contended that correlations between the various asset classes are not fixed and volatility is not constant over time. Others have asserted that investors should incorporate into their portfolios additional asset classes, which could be alternatives that were considered less traditional and/or conventional in the past.[227] Finally, the overlap of risk factors that might affect multiple asset classes also needs consideration. For example, international equities, emerging market equities and commodities might all be negatively impacted if the U.S. Dollar gets stronger. Also, if interest rates rise because of higher inflationary concerns, this will negatively impact a number of asset classes including bonds, stocks and perhaps to a lesser extent the U.S. Dollar.

In our view, the extent of the traditional role of bonds in a portfolio should be re-examined going forward. After a 30 plus year bull market in bonds, both private and sovereign, the potential end of this secular shift cannot be dismissed, particularly when factoring in both interest rates and outstanding debt levels. We do not necessarily believe an end to the secular bull market in bonds would create an automatic rush into equities and hence a subsequent bull market in stocks. Equity valuations may not necessarily be cheap if one subscribes to the Shiller 10 year normalized earnings measure. There are many seasoned money managers who feel that there could be a low return environment for both traditional equities and bonds for the intermediate future, especially in the developed regions of the world. One potential solution is to broaden the return and risk exposures in the portfolio by deploying strategies and asset classes outside the traditional stock and bond investments. There are many vehicles associated with alternatives. That said, maintaining a long term core allocation to equities and fixed income is a key tenet of MPT.

In conclusion, powerful arguments incorporating meaningful risk metrics such as consistency of returns, maximum draw downs, and downside volatility are important to building sustainable portfolios for different market cycles.

The Asset Allocation Value Proposition

Following is one of the most eloquent statements by Roger Gibson, author of *Asset Allocation, Balancing Financial Risk*, regarding the value of asset allocation:

> "Asset allocation is vitally important. The benefits of diversification are powerful and robust, not just in terms of volatility reduction but also for return enhancement. To evaluate the desirability of an asset class as a portfolio building block, it is not enough to know only its return and volatility characteristics. One must also know how its pattern of returns correlates to the patterns of returns of the other portfolio components. All other things being equal, the more dissimilarity there is among the patterns of returns of the asset classes within a portfolio, the stronger the diversification effect that provides investors with not only less volatility but also greater returns in the long run."[228]

When assessing an asset for inclusion in a portfolio, it is essential that the asset have the following properties. The asset should "earn its way" into the portfolio by being a source of long term returns and/or have some diversifying benefit that reduces volatility or risk.

Classic MPT-Based Asset Allocation

The original MPT based portfolios consisted of traditional assets only, mainly stocks, bonds, and cash. These portfolios were usually constructed as buy and hold strategies. Often with these strategies, the allocations were long-run and strategic in nature. The primary adjustments usually stemmed from rebalancing the portfolio. The next development was the "Tactical Asset Allocation Approach," which involved making periodic adjustments, beyond simple rebalancing, to the strategic allocations based on various proprietary models. The underlying theory is that one can add value to strategic asset allocations by "tilting." Tilting is the process of overweighting or underweighting certain asset classes that are deemed to be overvalued or undervalued. As an example, Solow and Kitces used a tactical asset allocation strategy using market valuations to decide when to make those allocations. Their basic thesis is that when bonds appear overvalued relative to equities, they adjust their allocation towards equities and vice versa.[229] While their methodology includes analyzing the relative valuation of equities to bonds, other methodologies focus on trend and momentum-based indicators such as moving averages.

Endowment Model Portfolio: MPT Version 3.0

Probably the best known non-traditional asset allocation strategy is the endowment model. Its origins began with the Ivy League Endowments, starting with Yale, Harvard and Stanford. They built their portfolios using the principles of traditional MPT such as diversification and mean variance optimization. Then they addressed some of the concerns of the post-MPT and MPT critics by adding alternative asset classes, such as private equity, real estate, hedge funds, managed futures, and commodities. Some of these asset classes were brought into portfolios to have a diversifying effect that reduced volatility. Other asset classes were introduced to enhance returns.

As a result of the 2007-2009 crash, these endowments, like many portfolios, were adversely affected. Some skeptics concluded that the endowment model was flawed if not broken. Others asserted that the endowment asset allocation model was fine, but poorly managed during the 2007 to 2009 crisis particularly with respect to liquidity risk.[230] In addition, some endowment model practitioners analyzing portfolio risk factors may have neglected to detect the duplication of risks across asset classes as occurred during the 2007 to 2009 economic crisis scenario.

In closing, our goal has not been to provide investment solutions. Instead our objective has been to build a conceptual framework within which one can begin approaching the world of investing.
Whether you believe in traditional MPT based portfolios or a modified version of MPT such as an endowment model approach, that is your decision. Bottom line, any of these approaches are good starting points from a portfolio construction stand point. They will help mitigate some of the typical emotions that investors experience during bear markets (fear) and bull markets (greed) and help them better navigate volatile markets.

MACROECONOMIC SCENARIO ANAYLSIS

Investopedia defines scenario analysis (not macroeconomic scenario analysis) as "the process of estimating the expected value of a portfolio after a given period of time, assuming specific changes in the values of the portfolios' securities or key factors that would affect security values, such as changes in the interest rate. Macroeconomic scenario analysis commonly focuses on estimating what a portfolio's value would be over time in response to a specific economic climate.

Figure 5-3 shows some key economic scenarios that have affected national and global economies over the last century. The Deflationary scenario is exemplified by two occurrences. In Japan, they are still experiencing deflationary conditions which began with a real estate bubble that collapsed in the early 1990's and has dragged on for two decades. We will explore the Japanese situation in more detail shortly. The United States experienced deflation during the Great Depression in the 1930's. The Ideal State: Goldilocks Economy occurred in the 1950s and early 60s after WW2 when there was strong growth and low/moderate inflation. The Stagflationary scenario happened during the 1970s, when the US experienced high/rising inflation and stagnant low growth exacerbated by the Oil Embargo and President Nixon abandoning the gold standard. An <u>Overheated Economy</u> in the 1990s had a period of rising economic growth and modest inflation (during the telecom and dot com bubble) that caused the economy to heat up.

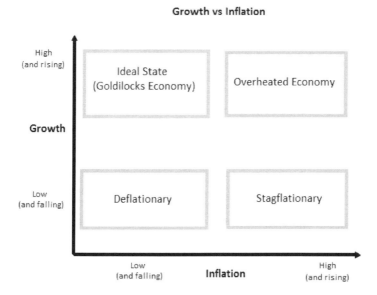

Figure 5-3: Growth vs. Inflation
Source: Courtesy of Neil Chakkera

This could also be referred to as a top down approach to economic analysis and investment decision making. In Francois Trahan's latest book, *The Era of Uncertainty: Global Investment Strategies for Inflation, Deflation, and the Middle Ground*, macro analysis and the importance of it is highlighted as the following:[231]

"Ignoring macro is like ignoring the seasons when trying to predict the weather. Any December day in New York City is likely to be a cold one. The "macro" backdrop indicates wearing a coat instead of shorts. The "stock specific" issues determine whether that coat should be a winter parka or a lighter jacket. It's possible to decide incorrectly on the choice of coat, but regardless one is usually better wearing a coat than shorts in December in New York City."[232].

Macroeconomic scenario analysis is a challenging undertaking. Given the large number of variables and uncertainties, many academics and investment professionals understandably view macroeconomic scenario planning efforts as unscientific and therefore unreliable. Our position is that even though there are tremendous challenges with this type of analytical exercise, there is still value in it when approached in the appropriate way. It's more of an art than science, but as time passes, macroeconomic scenario analysis will likely become more accepted as a useful analytical tool for making investment decisions.

Risk factor exposures include those that exist in traditional asset classes, such as stocks (equity risk), bonds (interest rate and credit risk), but also include others such as currencies, real estate, commodities and volatility. There are many more but for the purposes of this analysis we have focused on the four major risk factor exposures, which are as follows: equities, bonds, real assets and currencies. One resource for choosing these particular exposures is John Murphy, who has published extensively on the dynamics of Intermarket Analysis.[233]

Portfolio risk factor analysis is taking the aforementioned process one step further. One is not only trying to see how portfolio values will change as a result of one or two factor changes, such as interest rate movements or commodity price fluctuations, but how an entire portfolio might react to a multitude of factors that in turn are associated with a particular macroeconomic scenario. This 'scenario' is what Trahan refers to as the weather. According to his data, 71% of equity returns are explained by the economic climate. An extreme scenario would be a deflationary depression like the one in the United States in the 1930's. During those darkest days of U.S. economic history, interest rates plummeted, industrial activity came to a standstill, and commodity prices collapsed. In other words, there were a multitude of adverse changes in key risk factors that culminated in this unprecedented historical economic phenomenon. Understanding how a major economic event might impact a portfolio is the focus of risk factor analysis.

The end goal is the identification and understanding of aggregate risk factor exposures within an existing portfolio. Different types of investors will use the data generated in dissimilar ways. For example, the hedge manager may be seeking to opportunistically exploit market opportunities with this data. In contrast, a long term asset manager or professional investor may be using this analysis to identify additional ways of mitigating risk, reducing volatility or enhancing returns.

The next key step is to construct portfolios or adjust existing ones in a manner that is optimal given the economic scenario or scenarios that one anticipates materializing. Because there is rarely a clear cut path, one needs to have exposure to most asset classes. This is consistent with modern portfolio theory that sets forth the basic value proposition of diversification. Although we cannot foretell with 100% accuracy, which macroeconomic scenario will actually materialize, one can potentially overweight or underweight key asset classes or exposures that might behave favorably in a particular economic scenario that one has conviction will unfold in the foreseeable future.

SCENARIO 2, U SHAPED RECOVERY, JAPAN

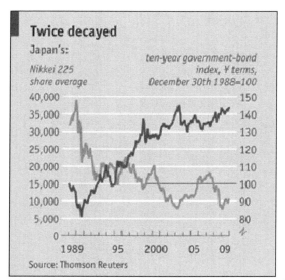

Figure 5-4: Japan's Ten Year Government – Bond Index 1987-2009
Source: Thomson Reuters

A good example of using a historical scenario to determine asset performance and risk factor analysis is Japan after their equity and housing bubbles burst. For our analysis, we looked at how key asset classes behaved during the 'lost decades' period. Key assets include sovereign bonds, equities, real estate, and the domestic currency. A 20+ year look back at Japanese stock performance shows how challenging this era was for equities. Conversely, sovereign bonds performed very strongly during the same time period. This would mirror the relative performance between stocks and treasury bonds in the U.S. during the Great Depression, a period somewhat similar to the Japanese experience. The interaction between these two asset classes in a deleveraging environment is expected.

The real estate market also was down significantly and then flat during the same period.

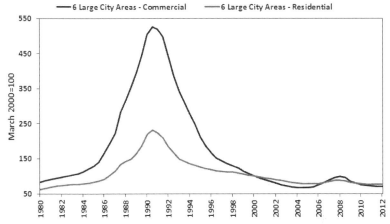

Figure 5-5: Japan Real Estate Price Index 1980-2012
Source: Japan Real Estate Institute

And lastly, the Japanese currency strengthened over this time period. Again these historic results not only shape our understanding of past performance, but also align well with our understanding of long term economic analysis and asset performance. In a primary deflationary trending environment, investors would expect to see weakening prices for equities and real estate, while sovereign bonds and domestic currency would likely strengthen. To counteract deflation, monetary authorities would normally be able to use their fractional reserve banking system to increase lending. This would increase money supply and credit thereby creating inflation. However when banks are deleveraging, that is, decreasing their debt levels, the money created by the monetary authority through the fractional reserve banking system isn't necessarily passed through to the greater economy, but is redirected to pay down debt. In other words, while money supply is increasing, the velocity of money is not, which does not help economic growth. Large secular shifts toward deleveraging tend to put long-term, downward pressure on asset prices. Conversely, during boom times, credit creation puts upward pricing pressure on those very same assets.

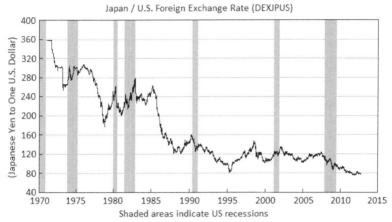

Figure 5-6: Japan/US Foreign Exchange Rate 1970-2015
Source: Federal Reserve Bank of St. Louis, grey areas are recession periods

Japan's situation can be readily understood and appreciated through a review of appropriate charts and graphs. This type of analysis can also be applied to the other four economic scenarios discussed in Chapter Four.

The foregoing analysis of Japan's U-shaped recovery from an economic viewpoint is a preliminary or early analysis. Since there are many differences amongst economies, simply taking past performance and directly applying it to another country, time frame, or region would not be accurate. Some of the major differences we discern between Japan and the U.S. include demographics, immigration policies, GDP composition, and, perhaps most importantly, currency status. We believe there is value in examining central bank policy, economic cycles, and overall macro factors impacting asset classes when building investment strategies. This type of thorough investigation will reveal how policy and country differences can modify the above macro factors. Thus, an analyst must probe beneath the superficial facts to discover the underlying 'climate' by accessing originating data bases, finding hidden or unrecognized economic interconnections, such as those between countries, and gaining a deeper understanding of economic and geo-political events.

		Macroeconomic Scenarios				
		One	Two	Three	Four	Five
		V Shaped Recovery	U Shaped Recovery	Recession	Depression	Hyperinflation
A s s e t C l a s s e s	Bonds	?	Positive	?	?	?
	Stocks	?	Negative	?	?	?
	Real Assets	?	Negative	?	?	?
	Currency	?	Positive	?	?	?

Figure 5-7: Macroeconomic Scenario Analysis Tool

Value of this Knowledge

The first step in using the Macroeconomic Scenario Analysis Tool in Figure 5-7 is to identify the economic scenario one wants to analyze. For our example, we'll use economic scenario 2, a "Japanese style" U shaped recovery that we analyzed in the previous section titled "SCENARIO 2, U SHAPED RECOVERY, JAPAN." The next step is to determine which risk factors affect or influence each of the four key asset classes in the case study above. Then we can attempt to aggregate the amount and type of risk factor exposures that impact equities, bonds, real estate and currency. If the net effect of the risk factor exposures for each asset class is meaningfully positive, we could put a "positive" next to that asset class for the U Shaped Recovery scenario in the Figure 5-7 or "negative," if the net effect is negative.

This type of analysis is also useful to evaluate an investor's existing portfolio to see how it might be invested in one or more of those asset classes. By understanding the aggregate risk factor exposures across the asset classes, the investor can determine if he or she is overexposed to a particular set of risk factors that might be unfavorable given the macroeconomic scenario that exists at that time. Imagine the value of a software application that decomposes the multiple risk factor exposures within a portfolio, which may consist of mutual funds, individual stocks, ETF's and aggregates those various account holdings into a single overall summary of risk factors.

During the Japanese U Shaped Recovery, Bond prices rose as Stocks declined and Japan's Currency strengthened. Thus, Bonds had an inverse correlation with Stocks and a high correlation with Japan's Currency. Hence having a framework to be able to over/underweight key asset classes proactively can potentially lead to better risk-adjusted investment outcomes over the market and economic cycle.

Different economic scenarios have meaningful and discernible impact on different asset classes. Is there any doubt that the prospect of or actual hyperinflation would drive commodities or real assets higher? Or for that matter, that deflation would help high quality bonds go up in value?

Non-institutional professional investors will look for software to guide them through the analyses we have described. However, based on our research of vendors and software packages, there do not appear to be many affordable products available. The good news is that we are seeing a tremendous amount of interest in this area and several established and new vendors are stepping in to fill this demand. We hope that risk analysis software that is affordable, user-friendly and accurate become available to the non-institutional investor in the near future.

CONCLUSION

The mountains of persistent debt in the advanced countries of the world, led by Japan, Europe, and the United States, are worrisome. Because of this debt, the sky could keep falling. Such is the nature of deleveraging. Some pundits such as Mary Meeker, a partner at Kleiner Perkins Caufield & Byers, project total federal government funded and unfunded liabilities of greater than $44 trillion, a staggering number to contemplate.[234] These debt chickens may come home to roost someday causing indebted governments to finally face the consequences.

Although high levels of inflation may take much longer to materialize than anticipated, several factors are contributing to a global inflationary bias. The Federal Reserve Bank is engaged in a combination of Operation Twist, Quantitative Easing and a low interest rate policy for as long as it takes employment to rise above acceptable levels. This is not just a domestic monetary policy. Other countries are counteracting this QE infinity, as the media is calling it, with inflationary policies of their own, capital flow restrictions into and out of their countries, foreign exchange currency interventions and trade restrictions on imports. As of this date, the total central bank balance sheets of 15 of the largest countries exceed $15 trillion. These "currency wars" are essentially trade wars of a "beggar thy neighbor" character wherein each country attempts to mitigate its economic problems at the expense of other countries. A current example of this is Japan's "Abenomics" monetary policy. In a zero sum game, Japan is purposely depreciating the Yen to boost their exports at the expense of other competitors such as Korea and China. In the United States, Congress has been raising budget spending caps to prevent what they consider the catastrophic effects of budget "sequestration," which would require automatic spending cuts by government agencies. In the Eurozone, the European Community Bank and the European central banks have been borrowing money by selling government bonds to bail out their indebted peripheral

143

nations: Spain, Greece, Ireland, Italy and Portugal. Japan has the greatest total and government debt to GDP ratios of any country. Their debt servicing capability could be severely tested if interest rates begin to rise. Japan's central bank, the Bank of Japan, is engaged in more money "printing" to offset the strengthening of the yen caused by the Fed's ongoing quantitative easing. All of the actions described in this paragraph are highly inflationary in the future and similar to fighting fire with fire or incurring additional debt to solve current debt problems, but it could all eventually end in a less than optimal manner.

Rather than referring to the fiscal cliff involving debt ceilings and sequestrations, we suggest using the term "fiscal slope," which is a trend that has been evolving over the last 40 or 50 years. In the previous chapters, we described the decades-long, downward drift in U.S. gross domestic product (GDP), the decreasing efficiency of each dollar of government stimuli to produce an increase in GDP, the parabolic increase in credit (debt), the dollar's steady loss of purchasing power and the latest financial crisis coupled with the Great Recession, which may not be the last or greatest economic meltdown.

The national and international factors that caused the Great Recession of 2007-2009 have not been eliminated. As we outlined in the previous chapters, we still have systemic risks that could trigger another financial crisis. The greatest danger is prohibitively high levels of debt here and abroad. As Rogoff and Reinhart have demonstrated in their classic book, *This Time Is Different: Eight Centuries of Financial Folly*, countries reach a tipping point when debt levels can no longer be sustained.[235] As long as countries "kick the can down the road," the sky could keep falling. Countries such as Greece have defaulted on their sovereign debt obligations. The question is, will we follow the path of nations such as Greece, Portugal, Spain or Italy or will we take the more difficult path following Ray Dalio's "beautiful deleveraging" involving debt reduction, austerity and the proper amount of debt monetization.[236]

For the advanced economies, the "End Game" to resolve debt issues will take different forms. Of most concern is Europe where the Eurozone crisis has reached a critical point. Attention needs to be focused on Japan, which has a debt to GDP ratio greater than 200%. If one factors in all debt including those of households, the debt to GDP ratio is 500%. Japan's economy has had extremely slow growth for over two decades partially due to an ever shrinking population. Japan's debt situation is a major accident waiting to happen. John Mauldin warns, "Japan is a bug in search of a windshield." If Japan's interest rates were to increase 2%, the interest on the national debt could exceed 80% of tax revenues or more.[237] If the markets react to the latter event, the ramifications would be dire.

As harsh as many of the underlying premises and conclusions of the book may be, it is our deepest wish that we as a country come through this crisis a stronger and better nation. However, given the unparalleled levels of debt in this country, executing any solution will be a tough, uphill battle. Unfortunately, when one looks at past history, both here and abroad, the resolve it takes to stay within budgets, whether at a national, state, or household level, has been an elusive goal. Excessive spending and funding shortfalls with more debt has been the usual panacea. We will have to make many hard choices to reach a happy ending. There is no magic bullet to solve years of expansive monetary and fiscal policy.

The good news is that people are beginning to understand the importance of getting our national, regional, and household debt back to manageable levels. The recent debt ceiling protests and fiscal cliff concerns attest to that fact. That said, if the drive towards 'austerity' actually gains traction, it could have serious deflationary implications for the U.S. and global economies. We can only hope for continued productive dialogue and actions that take us on a "glide path" to economic and financial stability.

Our goal has been to shed some light on how we got to where we are from a macroeconomic perspective. That started with identifying the appropriate thought leaders: economic analysts, economists, and financial professionals who were prescient enough to see the 2007-2009 crash coming. We look to these perceptive individuals for guidance on future developments, trends and market analysis. We have tried to provide many resources including books, articles and advisors' websites so you will be able to access their work directly. As authors, this has been a rewarding but challenging research project. You cannot determine where things are heading without first understanding where they were.

In Chapter Four, we set forth the different economic scenarios that could potentially develop. We have tried to identify the best spokespersons for each possible economic scenario. There were many others who deserved to be mentioned, but time and space prevented their inclusion. Our greatest conviction is that a lengthy period of deleveraging will ultimately end in an inflationary outcome. This inflation scenario may not appear for another three to seven years as Reinhart and Rogoff suggest from similar prior historical precedents. No matter what, we are in uncharted waters and it is difficult to gauge how long this low growth, anemic economic climate will continue. Which economic scenario emerges will likely depend most strongly on the type and level of government intervention that lies ahead of us.

Domestic and international monetary policies have made artificially low interest rates a mandate among central banks. The resulting excess liquidity has tended to seek higher returns through investments in risk assets. This in turn has inevitably led to bubbles in risk assets such as real estate, commodities or the stock market. These bubbles or market manias are characterized by high prices not supported by fundamentals. The resulting mal-investments inexorably lead to corrections or crashes when interest rates return to normal levels, the markets run out of buyers and income cannot sustain debt servicing. Will we experience deflation, stagflation, inflation or some other economic scenario? Only time will tell.

Lastly, by examining risk factor analysis, we provide a basic framework for investing in this unpredictable macroeconomic environment. By understanding the possible scenarios and their contributing factors, one can begin to see how different portions of a portfolio react to these external economic events.

In closing, we hope that as a country we heed the lessons of the past and take the proper actions leading to a brighter future.

RESOURCES

People Resources

Barnes, Martin H., Chief Economist, Managing Editor of Bank Credit Analyst, Web site: http://www.bcaresearch.com/

Dent, Harry S., President H.S. Dent Foundation and H.S. Dent Publishing, Newsletter: "HS Dent Monthly Economic Forecast," subscription, Web site: www.hsdent.com/.

Easterling, Ed: Founder Crestmont Research, Financial market education services and management of fund of hedge funds portfolio, Web site: http://www.crestmontresearch.com/.

El-Erian, Mohamed A.: CEO and co-CIO of Pacific Investment Management Company, Web site: http://www.pimco.com/en/Pages/default.aspx, Blog: "Secular Outlook."

Ferguson, Niall: Professor of History Harvard University, Web and Blog site: http://www.niallferguson.com/site/FERG/Templates/Home.aspx?pageid=1.

Gave, Loius-Vincent, CEO GaveKal, a financial services firm, Web site: http://gavekal.com/.

Grantham, Jeremy: Chief Investment Strategist of Grantham Mayo Van Otterloo (GMO), global investment management firm, Web and quarterly newsletter site: http://www.gmo.com/America/.

Gross, William H.: Managing Director and co-CIO of Pacific Investment Management Company, Web site: http://www.pimco.com/en/Pages/default.aspx, Blog: "Economic Outlook"

Howe, Neil: Historian, Economist, Demographer, Center for Strategic and International Studies, Web site: http://csis.org/.

Hoisington, Van R.: President and Senior Investment Officer of Hoisington Investment Management Company, Web site: http://www.hoisingtonmgt.com/, Newsletter: "Economic Overview" at http://www.hoisingtonmgt.com/hoisington_economic_overview.html.

Hunt, Lacy: Economist, Hoisington Investment Management Company, Web site: http://www.hoisingtonmgt.com/, Newsletter: "Economic Overview" at http://www.hoisingtonmgt.com/hoisington_economic_overview.html.

Krugman, Paul: Professor of Economics and International Affairs, Princeton University, Blog: "The Conscience of a Liberal" at http://krugman.blogs.nytimes.com , Nobel Memorial Prize in Economic Sciences.

Mauldin, John: Economic analyst, President, Millennium Wave Investments, Newsletters: "Thoughts from the Frontline" and "Outside the Box," Web site: http://www.investorsinsight.com/.

Peters, Don: Economist, Economic analyst, CPA, Chief Economic Strategist for Central Plains Advisors, Web site: http://www.centralplainsadvisors.com/.

Paulson, Jon: President of hedge fund Paulson & Company, which made $15 billion betting against the U.S. housing market.

Rajan, Raghuram: Professor of economics at University of Chicago, Blog: "Fault Lines," http://blogs.chicagobooth.edu/faultlines.

Rosenberg, David A., Chief Economist and Strategist at Gluskin Sheff, Newsletter: "Breakfast with Dave" at http://www.gluskinsheff.com/Research.aspx, subscription.

Roubini, Nouriel: Economist, Web site: www.roubini.com/ - Roubini Global Economics, Blog: http://www.rgemonitor.com/blog/roubini/, subscription.

Shiller, Robert: Professor of Economics at Yale University, Co-developer with Karl Case of Case-Shiller Home Price Indices, Web site: http://www.econ.yale.edu/~shiller/ and http://www.econ.yale.edu/~shiller/data.htm

Shilling, A. Gary: Economist, Financial analyst, 2010, Web site: http://www.agaryshilling.com/ Newsletter: "Insight Newsletter," subscription.

Taylor, John: Professor of Economics at Stanford University, Blog: http://www.johnbtaylorsblog.blogspot.com/.

Bibliography

Arrighi, Giovanni, *The Long Twentieth Century: Money, Power and the Origins of Our Times*, London and New York: Verso, 2010

Barker, David Knox, *The K Wave: Profiting from the Cyclical Booms and Busts in the Global Economy,* New York: Irwin Professional Publishing, 1995

Bryce, Robert, *Power Hungry: the myths of "green" energy and the real fuels of the future*, Jackson, Tennessee: PublicAffairs, 2011

Constable, Simon and Wright, Robert E., *The WSJ Guide to the 50 Economic Indicators That Really Matter: From Big Macs to "Zombie Banks," the Indicators Smart Investors Watch to Beat the Market*, HarperBusiness, Original edition, 2011

Dent, Harry, *The Great Depression Ahead : How to Prosper in the Crash Following the Greatest Boom in History*, New York: Free Press , 2008

Durbin, Michael, *All About Derivatives: The Easy Way To Get Started*, New York: McGraw-Hill, 2011

Duncan, Richard, *The New Depression: The Breakdown of the Paper Money Economy*, Singapore: John Wiley & Sons, 2012

Duncan, Richard, *The Corruption of Capitalism: A strategy to rebalance the global economy and restore sustainable growth*, CLSA Books, 2009

Duncan, Richard, *The Dollar Crisis: Causes, Consequences, Cures*, Singapore: John Wiley & Sons, 2005

Easterling, Ed, *Probable Outcomes: Secular Stock Market Insights*, Cypress House, 2011

Ferguson, Niall, *The Ascent of Money: A Financial History of the World*, Penguin (Non-Classics), 2009

Friedman, George, *The Next Decade: Where We've Been . . . and Where We're Going*, Doubleday, 2011

Friedman, Milton and Schwartz, Anna J., *A Monetary History of the United States, 1867-1960* Princeton: Princeton University Press, 1963

Gorton, Gary, *Slapped by the Invisible Hand: The Panic of 2007*, New York: Oxford University Press, 2010

Goyette, Charles, *The Dollar Meltdown : Surviving the Impending Currency Crisis with Gold, Oil, and Other Unconventional Investments*, Portfolio Hardcover, 2009

Hall, Thomas E. and Ferguson, J. David, *The Great Depression: an international disaster of perverse economic policies*, Ann Arbor, University of Michigan Press, 1998

Howe, Neil and Jackson, Richard, *The Graying of the Great Powers: Demography and Geopolitics in the 21st Century*, Washington, D.C.: Center for Strategic and International Studies, 2008

James, Lawrence, *The Rise and Fall of the British Empire*, New York, St. Martin's Press, 1997

Kennedy, Paul, *The Rise and Fall of the Great Powers: Economic Change and Military Conflict from 1500 to 2000*, New York: Random House, 1987

Kindleberger, Charles, *Manias, Panics, and Crashes*, New York: Palgrave Macmillan, sixth edition, 2011

Keynes, John Maynard, *General Theory of Employment, Interest and Money*, Eastford: Martino Fine Books, 2011

Koo, Richard C., *Balance Sheet Recession: Japan's Struggle with Uncharted Economics and its Global Implications*, John Wiley & Sons, 2003

Koo, Richard C., *The Holy Grail of Macroeconomics: Lessons from Japan's Great Recession*, Singapore, John Wiley & Sons, 2008

MacKay, David, "*Sustainable Energy — without the hot air,*" Version 3.5.2, November 3, 2008, download the free copy at http://www.withouthotair.com/

Mauldin, John and Tepper, Jonathan, *The Endgame: The End of the Debt Supercycle and How It Changes Everything*, Hoboken, NJ: John Wiley & Sons, 2011; *Bull's Eye Investing: Targeting Real Returns in a Smoke and Mirrors Market*, John Wiley & Sons, 2004

Murphy, John J., *Intermarket Analysis: Profiting from Global Market Relationships*, Hoboken, NJ: John Wiley and Sons, 2004

Prechter, Robert R., *Socionomics: The Science of History and Social Prediction*, Gainesville, New Classics Library, 2003

Rajan, Raghuram, *Fault Lines : How Hidden Cracks Still Threaten the World*, Princeton University Press, 2010

Rickards, James, *Currency Wars: The Making of the Next Global Crisis*, Penguin Group: London, England, 2011

Rogoff, Kenneth and Reinhart, Carmen, *This Time is Different: Eight Centuries of Financial Folly*, Princeton, Princeton University Press, 2009

Rothbard, Murray, *America's Great Depression*, Auburn, Alabama: The Ludwig Von Mises Institute, 2009

Roubini, Nouriel and Mihm, Stephen, *Crisis Economics: A Crash Course in the Future of Finance*, Penguin Press HC, 2010

Shiller, Robert J. and Akerlof, George A., *Animal Spirits: How Human Psychology Drives the Economy, and Why It Matters for Global Capitalism*, Princeton: Princeton University Press, 2010

Shiller, Robert, *Irrational Exuberance*, New York: Crown Business, 2006

Shilling, A. Gary, *The Age of Deleveraging: Investment Strategies for a Decade of Slow Growth and Deflation*, John Wiley & Sons, 2010

Trahan, Francois and Krantz, Katherine and Doll, Robert, *The Era of Uncertainty: Global Investment Strategies for Inflation, Deflation, and the Middle Ground*, Hoboken, NJ: John Wiley and Sons, 2011

Taylor, Dr. John, *Ending Government Bailouts as We Know Them* by Kenneth E. Scott, George P. Shultz and John B. Taylor, Hoover Institution Press, 1st edition, 2010

Web Sites

Bank for International Settlements, OTC derivatives market activity, http://www.bis.org/

Board of Governors of the Federal Reserve System, Economic Research & Data, http://www.federalreserve.gov/

Bureau of Economic Analysis (U.S. Department of Commerce), Economic data, http://www.bea.gov/

Congressional Budget Office, http://www.cbo.gov/

Economist magazine, http://www.economist.com/

Economist magazine's global debt clock: http://www.economist.com/content/global_debt_clock

EconoMonitor, Nouriel Roubini's blog, http://www.economonitor.com/

Federal Reserve Bank of St. Louis, Economic data and research,

http://research.stlouisfed.org/, FRED Graph,
http://research.stlouisfed.org/fred2/graph/

International Swaps and Derivatives Association, Over-the-counter
(OTC) derivatives markets, http://www2.isda.org/

MeasuringWorth, tracking dollar inflation and deflation over time,
http://www.measuringworth.com/

Ministry of Internal Affairs and Communication (Japan), Statistics
Bureau, Basic official Japanese statistics
http://www.stat.go.jp/english

National Bureau of Economic Research, De facto recession calls,
http://www.nber.org/

Office of the Comptroller of the Currency, Quarterly Reports on
Bank Trading and Derivatives Activities, http://www.occ.treas.gov/

Online Data - Robert Shiller,
http://www.econ.yale.edu/~shiller/data.htm

Options Clearing Corporation, Market Data on Volume, Open
Interest, and Series & Trading,
http://www.optionsclearing.com/market-data/

RealtyTrac, Foreclosure information, http://www.realtytrac.com/

TreasuryDirect, "The Debt to the Penny and Who Holds It,"
available at http://www.savingsbonds.gov/

U.S. Bureau of Labor Statistics, measuring labor market activity,
working conditions, and price changes in the economy,
http://data.bls.gov/

United States government debt clock:
http://www.usdebtclock.org/index.html

The World Factbook, Information on the history, people,
government, economy, geography, communications, transportation,
military, and transnational issues for 267 world entities,
https://www.cia.gov/library/publications/the-world-factbook/

Zillow, Real estate research, http://www.zillow.com

ENDNOTES

[1] *The Fortune Sellers: The Big Business of Buying and Selling Predictions*, William Sherden, Wiley, 1999, page 5

[2] Wikipedia, "Austrian School (Inflation)," available from http://en.wikipedia.org/wiki/Austrian_School#Inflation, accessed January 27, 2010

[3] Flow of Funds Accounts of the United States 1945 to 2010 Historical Data: http://www.federalreserve.gov/releases/z1/current/data.htm, Flow of Funds Accounts of the United States current data: http://www.federalreserve.gov/releases/z1/

[4] Wikipedia, Monetary Base, available at http://en.wikipedia.org/wiki/Monetary_base, accessed February 27, 2012

[5] Federal Bank of St. Louis, Fred Economic Data, St. Louis Adjusted Monetary Base (BASE), Excess Reserves of Depository Institutions (EXCRESNS), available at http://research.stlouisfed.org/fred2/, accessed February 27, 2012

[6] Flow of Funds Accounts of the United States 1945 to 2010 Historical Data: http://www.federalreserve.gov/releases/z1/current/data.htm, Flow of Funds Accounts of the United States current data: http://www.federalreserve.gov/releases/z1/

[7] Federal Bank of St. Louis, Fred Economic Data, Consumer Price Index for All Urban Consumers: All Items (CPIAUCSL), available at http://research.stlouisfed.org/fred2/, accessed February 27, 2012

[8] Federal Reserve statistical release, Z.1 Flow of Funds Accounts of the United States provide data for Total Credit Market Debt (TCMD) from Table L.1 Credit Market Debt Outstanding, Federal Reserve, Table 1 Money Stock Measures, end of year value from http://www.federalreserve.gov/releases/h6/hist/h6hist1.txt, not seasonally adjusted

[9] Federal Reserve Bank of St. Louis, Total Credit Market Debt Owed (TCMDO), available at http://research.stlouisfed.org/fred2/series/TCMDO, accessed April 7, 2012

[10] Federal Reserve, Table 1 Money Stock Measures, end of year value from

http://www.federalreserve.gov/releases/h6/hist/h6hist1.txt, not seasonally adjusted

[11] Richard Duncan, *The New Depression: The Breakdown of the Paper Money Economy*
Singapore: John Wiley & Sons, 2012, pgs 1-15

[12] Richard Duncan, *The New Depression: The Breakdown of the Paper Money Economy*
Singapore: John Wiley & Sons, 2012, pg ix

[13] Ellen Hodgson Brown, *The Web of Debt*, Baton Rouge, Louisiana: Third Millennium Press, December 2008, pgs 24-28

[14] Money What It Is How It Works, "Non-banks versus Banks," http://wfhummel.cnchost.com/nonbanks.html, accessed January 27, 2010

[15] The Fiscal Times, "What Can the Fed Do? Ending the subsidy to banks for not lending would help," Bruce Bartlett, available at http://www.thefiscaltimes.com/Columns/2010/07/23/What-Can-the-Fed-Still-Do.aspx on July 23, 2010, accessed on July 21, 2011

[16] Wikipedia, "Debt Monetization," available at http://en.wikipedia.org/wiki/Monetization, accessed June 19, 2012

[17] Board of Governors of the Federal Reserve System, Federal Reserve Statistical Release, Factors Affecting Reserve Balances, available at http://www.federalreserve.gov/releases/h41/, accessed July 19, 2011

[18] Central Intelligence Agency, *The World Factbook*, https://www.cia.gov/library/publications/the-world-factbook/rankorder/2187rank.html, accessed January 27, 2010

[19] Paul Kennedy, *The Rise and Fall of the Great Powers: Economic Change and Military Conflict from 1500 to 2000*, Random House, New York, 1987, pgs 536-537

[20] Professor Joseph Peden, Baruch College, *Inflation and the Fall of the Roman Empire*, Lecture given at the Seminar on Money and Government in Houston, Texas, October 27, 1984

[21] Wikipedia, "Crisis of the Third Century," http://en.wikipedia.org/wiki/Crisis_of_the_Third_Century, accessed on May 6, 2010

[22] Professor Joseph Peden, Inflation and the Fall of the Roman Empire, See endnote 9

[23] Wikipedia, "Crisis of the Third Century," See endnote 10

[24] Lawrence James, *The Rise and Fall of the British Empire*, St. Martin's Griffin, 1997, pgs 521-534

[25] Norris Arthur Brisco, "The Economic Policy of Robert Walpole," Columbia University Press, London, 1907, pgs 37-39

[26] Mises Wiki, "Public Debt," available at http://wiki.mises.org/wiki/Public_debt, accessed on February 19, 2012

[27] UK Public Spending, "Three Centuries of the National Debt," available at http://www.ukpublicspending.co.uk/uk_debt, accessed February 17, 2012

[28] Ibid.

[29] Bank of England, "UK Inflation 1790-2005," available at http://www.bankofengland.co.uk/education/inflation/timeline/chart.htm, accessed February 20, 2012

[30] Data Source is United Kingdom Office for National Statistics available at http://www.ons.gov.uk/ons/rel/cpi/consumer-price-indices/1750---2003/composite-consumer-price-index-with-description-and-assessment-of-source-data.pdf

[31] Lawrence James, *The Rise and Fall of the British Empire*, St. Martin's Griffin, 1997, pgs 521-534

[32] Bridgewater Associates, "Why Countries Succeed and Fail Economically©," Ray Dalio, available at http://www.bwater.com/Uploads/FileManager/research/deleveraging/why-countries-succeed-and-fail-economically--ray-dalio-bridgewater.pdf in June 2011, accessed March 21, 2012

[33] Wikipedia, "The world's first paper money," http://en.wikipedia.org/wiki/Chinese_currency, accessed January 31, 2010

[34] ePublish Yourself, Chapter 1 Gold for Iron, *When Money Dies - Nightmare of the Weimar Collapse*, Adam Fergusson, available at http://www.epubbud.com/read.php?g=JFXLC46C&p=3, accessed July 17, 2011

[35] Wikipedia, http://en.wikipedia.org/wiki/German_Reichsmark, accessed February 11, 2010

[36] National Monetary Commission, "The Reichsbank, 1876-1900, Volume 10," By Reichsbank (Berlin, Germany), United States, pg 70

[37] Prof. Dr. J. Welker, "Currency Developments," http://www.uni-saarland.de/fak1/fr12/welcker/CuDe.pdf, pg 15

[38] *The Great Depression: an international disaster of perverse economic policies*, Thomas E. Hall and J. David Ferguson, Ann Arbor: University of Michigan, 1998, pgs 77, 80

[39] The Concise Encyclopedia of Economics, *Great Depression*, Robert J. Samuelson, available from http://www.econlib.org/library/Enc1/GreatDepression.html, accessed February 3, 2010

[40] *The Great Depression: an international disaster of perverse economic policies*, Thomas E. Hall and J. David Ferguson, Ann Arbor: University of Michigan, 1998, pgs 116-117

[41] Wikipedia, "Gold exchange standard," available at http://en.wikipedia.org/wiki/Gold_standard#Post-war_international_gold-dollar_standard_.281946.E2.80.931971.29, accessed on February 28, 2012

[42] Time Magazine, *Bretton Woods System*, http://www.time.com/time/business/article/0,8599,1852254,00.html, M.J. Stephey, available Oct. 21, 2008, accessed February 15, 2010

[43] *The International Monetary Fund 1966-1971: The System Under Stress, Volume 1,* Margaret Garritsen De Vries, pgs 528-529

[44] U.S. Political History, Lyndon Baines Johnson (1963-1969), available at http://www.uspoliticalhistory.com/Johnson,_L._B._1.html, accessed March 20, 2012

[45] ibid, pgs 536-537

[46] Carmen Reinhart and Kenneth Rogoff, *This Time Is Different: Eight Centuries of Financial Folly* ©, Princeton University Press, Princeton, New Jersey, 2009, page 181

[47] Ludwig von Mises Institute, "Gold as Money: FAQ," available at http://mises.org/Community/wikis/economics/gold-as-money-faq.aspx on 12 August 2011, accessed February 26, 2012

[48] Freedom Daily, "Monetary Central Planning and the State, Part 27: Milton Friedman's Second Thoughts on the Costs of Paper Money," Richard M. Ebeling, available at http://www.fff.org/freedom/0399b.asp on February 1999, accessed February 27, 2012

[49] Ludwig von Mises, *The Causes of the Economic Crisis and Other Essays Before and After the Great Depression*, The Ludwig von Mises Institute, Auburn, Alabama, 1978, pgs. 69-70

[50] Ludwig von Mises, *The Theory of Money and Credit*, Yale University Press, New Haven, 1953, pg 396

[51] Wikipedia, "Fiat money," available at http://en.wikipedia.org/wiki/Fiat_currency, accessed February 10, 2012

[52] Friedman interview in The Guardian (London and Manchester), September 16, 1974

[53] Ludwig von Mises Institute, "Biography of Ludwig von Mises (1881-1973)," http://mises.org/page/1468/Biography-of-Ludwig-von-Mises-18811973, accessed February 21, 2012

[54] "Defense, Controls, and Inflation," A Conference Sponsored by the University of Chicago Law School, Edited by Aaron Director, page 109, available at http://mises.org/document/5863, accessed February 10, 2012

[55] Economagic, "CPI: U.S. City Average," available at http://www.economagic.com/blscu.htm, accessed on August 17, 2011

[56] The Wall Street Journal, "Deans List: Hiring Spree Fattens College Bureaucracy—And Tuition," Douglas Belkin and Scott Therm, December 29 – 30, 2012

[57] National Center for Policy Analysis, "Why Health Care Costs Are Still Rising," Devon Herrick, November 18, 2012, available at http://www.ncpa.org/pub/ba731, accessed on January 1, 2013

[58] Investopedia, "What Determines Gas Prices?" February 15, 2011, available at http://www.investopedia.com/articles/economics/08/gas-prices.asp#axzz2GkQgZCmJ, accessed January 1, 2013

[59] John Williams' Shadow Government Statistics, "No. 438—PUBLIC COMMENT ON INFLATION MEASUREMENT," April 8, 2013, available at http://www.shadowstats.com/article/no-438-public-comment-on-inflation-measurement, accessed January 1, 2013

[60] Ibid.

[61] Economics One, Stanford University, "What Does Anti-Keynesian Mean?" A Blog by John B. Taylor, available at http://johnbtaylorsblog.blogspot.com/2011/07/what-does-anti-keynesian-mean.html on July 19, 2011, accessed on September 5, 2011

[62] Hoover Institution, Where Did the Stimulus Go?" John F. Cogan and John B. Taylor, available at http://media.hoover.org/sites/default/files/documents/Where-Did-Stimulus-Go-Commentary-1-2011.pdf on January 2011, accessed September 5, 2011

[63] The Wall Street Journal, "Why Permanent Tax Cuts Are the Best Stimulus," Opinion by John B. Taylor, available at

http://online.wsj.com/article/SB122757149157954723.html on
November 25, 2008, accessed September 5, 2011

[64] Kenneth Rogoff and Carmen Reinhart, *This Time is Different:
Eight Centuries of Financial Folly*, Princeton, NJ: Princeton
University Press, 2009, pg 142

[65] Vox, "Growth in a Time of Debt," Kenneth Rogoff and Carmen
Reinhart, available at
http://www.voxeu.org/index.php?q=node/5395 on August 11,
2010, accessed October 9, 2010

[66] Investopedia, "K-Percent Rule, available at
http://www.investopedia.com/terms/k/k-percent-
rule.asp#axzz1WH8ThNWY, accessed August 27, 2011

[67] Library of Economics and Liberty, An Interview with Milton
Friedman, Russell Roberts, available at
http://www.econlib.org/library/Columns/y2006/Friedmantranscript.
html on September 4, 2006, accessed February 11, 2012

[68] Milton Friedman and Anna J. Schwartz, *A Monetary History of
the United States, 1867-1960* (Princeton, NJ: Princeton University
Press for the NBER, 1963), chapter 5, pp. 231-239.

[69] Murray N. Rothbard, "Milton Friedman Unraveled," Journal of
Libertarian Studies, Fall 2002

[70] Milton Friedman, Presidential address at Western Economic
Association, "Economists and Economic Policy," available at
http://0055d26.netsolhost.com/friedman/pdfs/wsj/WSJ.01.22.2007.
pdf on July 1985

[71] NATIONAL BUREAU OF ECONOMIC RESEARCH, "NEW
KEYNESIAN VERSUS OLD KEYNESIAN GOVERNMENT
SPENDING MULTIPLIERS," Working Paper 14782, John F.
Cogan, Tobias Cwik, John B. Taylor, and Volker Wieland,
available at
http://harrisdellas.net/conferences/hydra09/papers/nber-
w14782.pdf on March 2009, accessed September 12, 2011

[72] Wall Street Journal Online, "Government Spending Is No Free
Lunch," available at
http://online.wsj.com/article/SB123258618204604599.html, Robert
J. Barro, January 22, 2009, accessed on May 25, 2010

[73] Mises Daily, "The Origin of the Income Tax," The Origin of the
Income Tax," Adam Young, available from
http://mises.org/daily/1597 on September 7, 2010, accessed
November 23, 2010

[74] www.voxeu.org, "Design and effectiveness of fiscal-stimulus programmes," available at http://www.voxeu.org/index.php?q=node/4144, Robert Barro and Charles Redlick, 30 October 2009, accessed on May 26, 2010

[75] The Wall Street Journal, "Why Permanent Tax Cuts Are the Best Stimulus," John B. Taylor, available at http://online.wsj.com/article/SB122757149157954723.html on November 25, 2011, accessed September 25, 2011

[76] Wikipedia, "Price Revolution," available at http://en.wikipedia.org/wiki/Price_revolution, accessed March 24, 2012

[77] Milton Friedman, "The Case for Flexible Exchange Rates," in Essays in Positive Economics, Chicago: University of Chicago Press, 1953, pp. 157-203

[78] Wikipedia, "Balance of Trade," available at http://en.wikipedia.org/wiki/Balance_of_trade, accessed on September 20, 2011

[79] The Phora, "World Economy in Flux As America Downshifts," Michael M. Phillips, available at http://www.thephora.net/forum/archive/index.php/t-29334.html on September 20, 2007, accessed September 20, 2011

[80] Milton Friedman @ Rest Email from a Nobel Laureate, available at http://www.opinionjournal.com/extra/?id=110009561, WSJ Opinion Archives, January 22, 2007, accessed March 11, 2010

[81] Cato Institute, "Milton Friedman: Float or Fix?" Steve H. Hanke, available at http://www.cato.org/pubs/journal/cj28n2/cj28n2-11.pdf on September 2, 2008, accessed August 10, 2012

[82] About.com, a part of The New York Times Company, "Quantitative Easing," Kimberly Amadeo, available at http://useconomy.about.com/od/glossary/g/Quantitative-Easing.htm, accessed on August 27, 2011

[83] Wikipedia, "Quantitative Easing," available at http://en.wikipedia.org/wiki/Quantitative_easing, accessed on December 29, 2012

[84] The Economist, "How to stop a currency war," available on http://www.economist.com/node/17251850 from October 14, 2010, accessed on November 7, 2010

[85] James Rickards, Currency Wars: The Making of the Next Global Crisis, Penguin Group: London, England, 2011, 56-97, 100

[86] EconoMonitor, "States of Risk," Nouriel Roubini, available at http://www.economonitor.com/nouriel/2010/03/17/states-of-risk/ on March 17, 2010, accessed September 19, 2011

[87] EconoMonitor, "Roubini Crisis Economics Q&A with Ian Bremmer on Amazon," Nouriel Roubini, available at http://www.economonitor.com/nouriel/2010/04/26/roubini-crisis-economics-qa-with-ian-bremmer-on-amazon/ on April 10, 2010, accessed September 19, 2011

[88] Nouriel Roubini and Stephen Mihm, *Crisis Economics*, Penguin Press HC, 2010, pg 19

[89] United Nations Conference on Trade and Development, "Trade and Development Report 2009, Chapter IV Reform of the International Monetary and Financial System" available at http://archive.unctad.org/templates/webflyer.asp?docid=11867&intItemID=1397&lang=1&mode=toc, http://archive.unctad.org/en/docs/tdr2009ch4_en.pdf accessed July 31, 2012

[90] International Monetary Fund, "Reserve Accumulation and International Monetary Stability," Strategy, Policy and Review Department, Approved by Reza Moghadam, available at http://www.imf.org/external/np/pp/eng/2010/041310.pdf on April 13 2010, accessed July 31, 2012, pgs 2-3, 26-28

[91] International Monetary Fund, "Reserve Accumulation and International Monetary Stability: Supplemental Information," Strategy, Policy and Review Department, Approved by Reza Moghadam, available at http://www.imf.org/external/np/pp/eng/2010/041310a.pdf on April 13 2010, accessed August 11, 2012, pgs 14-15

[92] Financial Times, "The G20 must look beyond Bretton Woods II," Robert Zoellick, available at http://www.ft.com/intl/cms/s/0/5bb39488-ea99-11df-b28d-00144feab49a.html#axzz23GSnBSqg on November 7, 2010, accessed August 11, 2012

[93] John Taylor, *Getting Off Track: How Government Actions and Interventions Caused, Prolonged, and Worsened the Financial Crisis*, Stanford, California, Hoover Institution Press, 2009, page 67

[94] Ibid. pgs 1-3

[95] Ibid. pgs 4-5

[96] U.S. Census Bureau, "New Privately Owned Housing Units Started - Seasonally Adjusted Annual Rate," available at

http://www.census.gov/const/startssa.pdf, accessed August 29, 2011

[97] John Taylor, *Getting Off Track: How Government Actions and Interventions Caused, Prolonged, and Worsened the Financial Crisis*, Stanford, California, Hoover Institution Press, 2009, page 62

[98] Federal Reserve Bank of New York, Reducing Systemic Risk in a Dynamic Financial System, available from http://www.newyorkfed.org/newsevents/speeches/2008/tfg080609.html on June 9, 2008, accessed June 24, 2010

[99] University of Maryland, American Enterprise Institute, "After the Fall," Carmen Reinhart and Vincent R. Reinhart, available at http://www.carmenreinhart.com/user_uploads/AftertheFall_August_27_NBER.pdf on August 2010, accessed March 22, 2012

[100] George A. Akerlof and Robert J. Shiller, *Animal Spirits: How Human Psychology Drives the Economy, and Why It Matters for Global Capitalism*, Princeton University Press, 2010

[101] Wikipedia, "Austrian business cycle theory," available at http://en.wikipedia.org/wiki/Austrian_business_cycle_theory, accessed Julyu 20, 2012

[102] Wikipedia, "John Maynard Keynes," available at http://en.wikipedia.org/wiki/John_Maynard_Keynes, accessed July 21, 2012

[103] Wikipedia, "Credit Cycle," available at http://en.wikipedia.org/wiki/Credit_cycle, accessed July 21, 2012

[104] George A. Akerlof and Robert J. Shiller, *Animal Spirits: How Human Psychology Drives the Economy, and Why It Matters for Global Capitalism*, Princeton University Press, 2010

[105] Federal Reserve Bank of St. Louis, Total Credit Market Debt Owed (TCMDO), available at http://research.stlouisfed.org/fred2/series/TCMDO, accessed April 7, 2012

[106] Richard Duncan, *The New Depression: The Breakdown of the Paper Money Economy* Singapore: John Wiley & Sons, 2012, pg66

[107] Ibid., pgs 33, 42, 43

[108] Verso, *The Long Twentieth Century: Money, Power and the Origins of Our Times*, Giovanni Arrighi, 2010, 2nd edition, pgs ix, 6

[109] Ibid. pgs 14-18

[110] EconoMonitor, "Roubini Yahoo! Finance Interviews: Europe's Contagion 'Has Now Gone Viral…and Global' While U.S.

Government Gridlock 'Ensures' 2012 Recession," Nouriel Roubini, available at http://www.economonitor.com/nouriel/2011/11/23/roubini-yahoo-finance-interviews-europe%e2%80%99s-contagion-has-now-gone-viral%e2%80%a6and-global-while-u-s-government-gridlock-%e2%80%98ensures%e2%80%99-2012-recession/ on November 23, 2011, accessed on December 8, 2011

[111] National Bureau of Economic Research, "After the Fall," Carmen M. Reinhart and Vincent R. Reinhart, available on August 2010 at http://www.kansascityfed.org/publicat/sympos/2010/2010-08-17-reinhart.pdf, accessed on January 14, 2011

[112] According to the OECD, Debt Service Ratio is defined as the ratio of debt service payments made by or due from a country to that country's export earnings.

[113] Kleiner Perkins Caufield & Byers, "A Basic Summary of Americas' Financial Statements," Mary Meeker, available at http://www.kpcb.com/usainc/USA_Inc.pdf on February 2011, accessed September 22, 2100

[114] Organisation for Economic Co-operation and Development

[115] Bank for International Settlements, "The future of public debt: prospects and implications," Stephen G Cecchetti, M S Mohanty, and Fabrizio Zampolli, March 2010

[116] Bank for International Settlements, Monetary and Economic Department, "The real effects of debt," Stephen G. Cecchetti, M. S. Mohanty and Fabrizio Zampolli, available at http://www.bis.org/publ/work352.pdf on September 2011, accessed November 3, 2011

[117] International Monetary Fund, "World Economic outlook: Growth Resuming, Dangers Remain," available at http://www.imf.org/external/pubs/ft/weo/2012/02/index.htm on October 2012 2012, accessed March 18, 2012

[118] Ibid.

[119] European Central Bank, "Long-term interest rate statistics for EU Member States," available at http://www.ecb.int/stats/money/long/html/index.en.html, Long-term interest rate data: Download CSV, accessed June 22, 2012

[120] European Central Bank, "Long-term interest rate statistics for EU Member States," available at http://www.ecb.int/stats/money/long/html/index.en.html, Long-term interest rate data: Download CSV, accessed June 22, 2012

[121] Wikipedia, " European sovereign-debt crisis," available at http://en.wikipedia.org/wiki/European_sovereign-debt_crisis, accessed January 1, 2013

[122] American Economic Review Papers and Proceedings, "Growth in a Time of Debt," Kenneth Rogoff and Carmen Reinhart, January 7, 2010

[123] Congressional Budget Office, "The Budget and Economic Outlook: An Update," available from http://www.cbo.gov/sites/default/files/cbofiles/attachments/08-22-2012-Update_to_Outlook.pdf, accessed January 4, 2013

[124] Bank for International Settlements, Monetary and Economic Department, "The real effects of debt," Stephen G. Cecchetti, M. S. Mohanty and Fabrizio Zampolli, available at http://www.bis.org/publ/work352.pdf on September 2011, accessed November 3, 2011

[125] Bloomberg Businessweek, "When Debt Stifles Growth," Carmen M. Reinhart and Kenneth S. Rogoff, available at http://www.businessweek.com/magazine/when-debt-stifles-growth-07142011.html on July 14, 2011, accessed October 28, 2011

[126] The Economist magazine, "World debt guide," available at http://www.economist.com/gallery/2012-05-02/world-debt-guide on July 28 2011, accessed on December 23, 2011

[127] Financial Sense, "When Default is a Mathematical Certainty," Dr. John Hussman, Hussman Funds, available at http://www.financialsense.com/contributors/john-hussman/2011/07/25/when-default-is-a-mathematical-certainty on July 25, 2011, accessed December 27, 2011

[128] National Bureau of Economic Research, "After the Fall," Carmen M. Reinhart and Vincent R. Reinhart, available on August 2010 at http://www.kansascityfed.org/publicat/sympos/2010/2010-08-17-reinhart.pdf, accessed on January 14, 2011, pg 23

[129] Alternative measure of labor underutilization U-6 - LNS13327709 and Labor Force Statistics from the Current Population Survey, U.S. Bureau of Labor Statistics, available at http://data.bls.gov/cgi-bin/surveymost?ln, accessed March 17, 2012

[130] Organisation for Economic Co-operation and Development (OECD), "Small Businesses, Job Creation and Growth: Facts, Obstacles and Best Practices," 1997, accessed August 18, 2010

[131] Federal Reserve Bank of New York, "National Economy, data available at"

http://www.newyorkfed.org/research/national_economy/index.html
, accessed August 12, 2012

[132] "WHY THE U.S. NEED NOT FEAR A SOVEREIGN DEBT CRISIS:
UNLIKE GREECE, IT IS ACTUALLY SOVEREIGN," Ellen Brown, available at
http://www.webofdebt.com/articles/greece_skids.php on July 22, 2010, accessed December 12, 2010

[133] Economix Blog, The New York Times, "Fearing (Another) U.S. Debt Default," CATHERINE RAMPELL, available on
http://economix.blogs.nytimes.com/2011/01/04/fearing-another-u-s-debt-default/ on January 4, 2011, accessed on January 21, 2011

[134] Vox, "Eight hundred years of financial folly," Carmen M. Reinhart, available at
http://www.voxeu.org/index.php?q=node/1067 on 5 May 2010, accessed on January 21, 2011

[135] Federal Reserve Bank of New York, "Currency Devaluation and Revaluation," available at
http://www.newyorkfed.org/aboutthefed/fedpoint/fed38.html, accessed on January 21, 2011

[136] Der Spiegel, The Disastrous Consequences of a Euro Crash," available at http://www.spiegel.de/international/europe/fears-grow-of-consequences-of-potential-euro-collapse-a-840634.html on June 25, 2012, accessed July 5, 2012

[137] Ibid.

[138] Bloomberg News, "Greece Deal Triggers $3B in Default Swaps: ISDA," Abigail Moses and Mary Childs, available at
http://www.businessweek.com/news/2012-03-09/greek-debt-deal-might-trigger-3-billion-of-default-swaps-under-isda-rules on March 9, 2012, accessed March 11,2012

[139] Investors Insight, Thoughts From The Frontline, "The Debt Supercycle," John Mauldin, available from
http://www.investorsinsight.com/blogs/thoughts_from_the_frontline/archive/2010/07/17/the-debt-supercycle.aspx on July 17, 2010, accessed on September 12, 2010

[140] Barry Eichengreen: University of California, Berkeley, Kris Mitchener: Santa Clara University, "The Great Depression as a Credit Boom Gone Wrong," available at
http://emlab.berkeley.edu/~eichengr/research/bisconferencerevision5jul30-03.pdf in August 2003, accessed April 12, 2012

[141] Ludwig von Mises, *Human Action*, Ludwig von Mises Institute, Auburn, Alabama, 1998 (originally published in 1949), page 570

[142] CNBC-TV video, "Bond Vigilantes and the US," available at http://207.46.150.45/id/15840232?video=1773717046&play=1 on January 31, 2011, accessed March 21, 2011

[143] Wikipedia, "Government bond," available at http://en.wikipedia.org/wiki/Sovereign_bond, accessed on March 22, 2012

[144] National Affairs, "Inflation and Debt," John H. Cochrane, available at http://faculty.chicagobooth.edu/john.cochrane/research/papers/Cochrane_Inflation_and_Debt_National_Affairs.pdf Fall 2011, accessed March 29, 2012

[145] Harvard University of Economics, Debt Overhangs: Past and Present," Carmen M. Reinhart, Vincent R. Reinhart and Kenneth Rogoff, available at http://www.economics.harvard.edu/faculty/rogoff/Recent_Papers_Rogoff/ on April 15, 2012, accessed July 27, 2012

[146] Bank for International Settlements, " Table 19: Amounts outstanding of over-the-counter (OTC) derivatives by risk category and instrument," available at http://www.bis.org/statistics/otcder/dt1920a.pdf on June 2012, accessed June 23, 2012

[147] Bloomberg, "U.S. Banks Aren't Nearly Ready for Coming European Crisis," Simon Johnson, available at http://www.bloomberg.com/news/2012-06-24/u-s-banks-aren-t-nearly-ready-for-coming-european-crisis.html on June 24, 2012, accessed August 17, 2012

[148] Office of the Comptroller of the Currency, "OCC's Quarterly Report on Bank Trading and Derivatives Activities Third Quarter 2012," available at http://www.occ.gov/topics/capital-markets/financial-markets/trading/derivatives/dq312.pdf, accessed January 2, 2013

[149] Project Syndicate, "Countering the Contagious West," Mohamed A. El-Erian, available at http://www.project-syndicate.org/commentary/elerian9/English on September 19, 2011, accessed September 22, 2011

[150] Ibid.

[151] European Financial Stability Facility (EFSF), "About EFSF," available at http://www.efsf.europa.eu/about/index.htm in May 2010, accessed November 11, 2011

[152] Wikipedia, "European Financial Stability Mechanism" available at http://en.wikipedia.org/wiki/European_Financial_Stability_Mechanism, accessed January 3, 2013

[153] Wikipedia, "European Stability Mechanism," available at http://en.wikipedia.org/wiki/European_Stability_Mechanism, accessed January 3, 2013

[154] Investors Insight, Thoughts From The Frontline, "Where is the ECB Printing Press?," John Mauldin, available from http://www.investorsinsight.com/blogs/thoughts_from_the_frontline/archive/2011/11/12/where-is-the-ecb-printing-press.aspx on November 12, 2011, accessed on September 15, 2011

[155] Yahoo Finance, The Daily Ticker, "Robert Shiller: A Housing Bottom? What Are They Thinking?" available at http://finance.yahoo.com/blogs/daily-ticker/robert-shiller-housing-bottom-thinking-134116144.html;_ylt=Amhmh.8qji_v2f99bRaorucp2YdG;_ylu=X3oDMTFpOWt2Y3VjBG1pdANCbG9nIFBvc3QgQm9keQRwb3MDNgRzZWMDTWVkaWFCbG9nQm9keUFzc2VtYmx5;_ylg=X3oDMTNmYmVwaWVyBGludGwDdXMEbGFuZwNlbi11cwRwc3RhaWQDZGJjZmZiZmEtOGIyZC0zYWQwLWFhZmMtMtY2UxZGYyOWZhMDY2BHBzdGNhdANleGNsdXNpdmVzfGRhaWWx5dGlja2VyBHB0A3N0b3J5cGFnZQR0ZXN0Aw--;_ylv=3 on January 30, 2012, accessed February 3, 2012

[156] NATIONAL BUREAU OF ECONOMIC RESEARCH, Working Paper 16893, "THE LIQUIDATION OF GOVERNMENT DEBT, Carmen M. Reinhart and M. Belen Sbrancia, available at http://www.imf.org/external/np/seminars/eng/2011/res2/pdf/crbs.pdf on March 2011, accessed August 6, 2011, pgs 46-47

[157] Ibid.

[158] Bridgewater Associates, "An In Depth Look at Deleveragings©," Ray Dalio, available at http://sz0121.ev.mail.comcast.net/service/home/~/Deleveraging-ray-dalio-bridgewater.2012pdf.pdf?auth=co&loc=en_US&id=215520&part=2 in February 2012, accessed April 4, 2012

[159] Ibid.

[160] Bank for international Settlements, "The Great Depression as a credit boom gone wrong," BIS Working Papers No 137, Barry Eichengreen, University of California, Berkeley, and Kris

Mitchener, Santa Clara University, Monetary and Economic Department, available at http://www.bis.org/publ/work137.pdf on September 2003, accessed April 26, 2012, pgs 36-38

[161] National Bureau of Economic Research, "Securitization in the 1920s," available at http://www.nber.org/digest/may10/w15650.html, accessed May 1, 2012

[162] Credit Suisse, "Twice a Century Deleveraging?" James Sweeney, available at https://infocus.credit-suisse.com/app/article/index.cfm?fuseaction=OpenArticle&aoid=3 19037&lang=EN on December 9, 2012, accessed on May 2, 2012

[163] SNL Financial, "2013 — the year of the leverage ratio," David Brierley and Saad Sarfraz, available at http://www.snl.com/InteractiveX/Article.aspx?cdid=A-16673625-13096 on December 21, 2012, accessed on January 10, 2013

[164] Princeton University, Moody's Analytics, "How the Great Recession Was Brought to an End," Alan S. Blinder and Mark Zandi, available at http://www.economy.com/mark-zandi/documents/End-of-Great-Recession.pdf on July 27, 2010, accessed April 3, 2011

[165] Remarks by Governor Ben S. Bernanke Before the National Economists Club, Washington, D.C. November 21, 2002, "Deflation: Making Sure "It" Doesn't Happen Here," available at http://www.federalreserve.gov/boarddocs/speeches/2002/20021121/default.htm on November 2002, accessed on October 5, 2011

[166] Ibid.

[167] Ibid.

[168] CNNMoney, Federal Reserve launches Operation Twist, Annalyn Censky, available at http://money.cnn.com/2011/09/21/news/economy/federal_reserve_operation_twist/index.htm on September 22, 2011, accessed October 7, 2011

[169] Gluskin Sheff, Market Musings & Data Deciphering, David A. Rosenberg, Chief Economist & Strategist, July 23, 2010

[170] PIMCO, "The Shadow Banking System and Hyman Minsky's Economic Journey," available from PIMCO May 2009, Paul McCulley, accessed July 27, 2010

[171] Yahoo Tech Ticker, Obama Falls Short; Gary Shilling Sees 10 Years of Low Growth + Rising Unemployment, available http://finance.yahoo.com/tech-ticker/obama-falls-short-gary-

shilling-sees-10-years-of-low-growth--rising-unemployment-535322.html;_ylt=AlvPRZeNZDzXdCHr73MY0tdk7ot4;_ylu=X3 oDMTE4ZGtxcmZxBHBvcwMxNzkEc2VjA2FydGljbGVVMaXN0 BHNsawNvYmFtYWZhbGxzc2g-?tickers=%5EDJI,%5EGSPC,TBT,TLT,UUP,UDN,XLF August 12, 2010, accessed August 26, 2010

[172] InvestorsInsight Publishing, "Absolute Zero," excerpt from A. Gary Shilling's INSIGHT, available at http://www.investorsinsight.com/blogs/john_mauldins_outside_the_box/archive/2011/09/26/absolute-zero.aspx on September 26, 2011, accessed October 5, 2011

[173] Daily Finance, "Japan's Cheap Debt Could Cost the World Dearly," Charles Hugh Smith, available http://www.dailyfinance.com/story/investing/japans-cheap-debt-could-cost-the-world-plenty/19579257/ August 4, 2010, accessed September 1, 2010

[174] Center for Strategic and International Studies, "The Age of Balance Sheet Recessions: What Post-2008 U.S., Europe and China Can Learn from Japan 1990-2005," Richard C. Koo available from http://csis.org/files/media/csis/events/090326_koo_presentation.pdf , March 2009, accessed September 1, 2010

[175] *Balance Sheet Recession: Japan's Struggle with Uncharted Economics and its Global Implications*, Richard C. Koo, Wiley, 2003

[176] *The Holy Grail of Macroeconomics: Lessons from Japan's Great Recession*, Richard C. Koo, Wiley & Sons, 2008

[177] Ministry of Finance, "Highlights of the Budget for FY2012," available at http://www.mof.go.jp/english/budget/budget/fy2012/e20111224a.pdf, December 2011, accessed January 11, 2012

[178] The Atlantic Magazine, "The Next Game," Peter Boone and Simon Johnson, October 2012, available at http://www.theatlantic.com/magazine/archive/2012/10/the-next-panic/309081/?single_page=true, accessed on January 11, 2013

[179] Japan Ministry of Internal Affairs and Communications, Statistics Bureau, *Statistical Handbook of Japan 2009*, Chapter 2 Population

[180] CNNMoney, "Rising GDP Doesn't Rule Out Recession," Lakshman Achuthan and Anirvan Banerji, Economic Cycle Research Institute,

http://money.cnn.com/2012/05/11/news/economy/achutan-recession/, May 1, 2012, accessed May 19, 2012

[181] Economic Cycle Research Institute, "The Tell-Tale Chart," available at http://www.businesscycle.com/ecri-news-events/news-details/economic-cycle-research-us-recession-start on December 7, 2012, accessed January 11, 2012

[182] Project Syndicate, "The Economic Fundamentals of 2013," Nouriel Roubini, available at http://www.project-syndicate.org/commentary/the-global-economy-s-rising-risks-in-2013-by-nouriel-roubini on January 21, 2013, accessed January 23, 2013

[183] Hussman Funds, "Brief Holiday Update ," available at http://www.hussman.net/wmc/wmc121231.htm on December 31, 2012, accessed January 12, 2013

[184] Hussman Funds, "How to Build a Time Machine," available at http://www.hussman.net/wmc/wmc121203.htm on December 3, 2012, accessed January 12, 2013

[185] Wikipedia, "Quantitative Easing," available from http://en.wikipedia.org/wiki/Quantitative_easing, accessed September 27, 2010

[186] ABC News, "IMF warns recession risk 'alarmingly high'," available at http://www.abc.net.au/news/2012-10-09/imf-lowers-growth-forecast/4302666 on October 9, 2012, accessed January 11, 2013

[187]

http://www.oecd.org/newsroom/globaleconomyfacinghesitantandunevenrecoverysaysoecd.htm

[188] Business Insider, "ROSENBERG: A Crucial Economic Indicator Just Sank To A Level That Coincides With Recession 100% Of The Time," Sam Ro, available at http://www.businessinsider.com/rosenberg-core-capex-orders-recession-2012-9 September 29, 2012, accessed January 12, 2012

[189] The Economist, "Diagnosing depression: What is the difference between a recession and a depression?" available at http://www.economist.com/node/12852043 on December 30, 2008, accessed March 19, 2011

[190] The Daily Ticker, "We Are Living in a 'Modern-Day Depression': David Rosenberg," Aaron Task, available at http://finance.yahoo.com/blogs/daily-ticker/living-modern-day-depression-david-rosenberg-121332909.html on June 25, 2012, accessed June 25, 2012

[191] Richard Duncan, *The New Depression: The Breakdown of the Paper Money Economy* Singapore: John Wiley & Sons, 2012, Chapter 8 Disaster Scenarios, pg 121

[192] Ibid. pgs 126-127

[193] Ibid. pgs 126-128

[194] Bloomberg, "U.S. Property Owners Lost $3.3 Trillion in Home Value," Dan Levy, available from http://www.bloomberg.com/apps/news?pid=newsarchive&sid=aE29HSrxA4rI&refer=home on February 3, 2009, accessed September 4, 2010

[195] PIMCO Investment Outlook, "Privates Eye," Bill Gross, available from http://www.pimco.com/Pages/PrivatesEyeBillGrossAugust2010.aspx on August 2010, accessed September 9, 2010

[196] Harry S. Dent, *The Great Depression Ahead*, Free Press, New York, 2008, pgs 44-46

[197] Ibid, pg 178

[198] Federal Reserve Bank of St. Louis, The Debt-Deflation Theory of Great Depressions, Irving Fisher, 1912, available at http://fraser.stlouisfed.org/docs/meltzer/fisdeb33.pdf

[199] Wikipedia, Hyman Minsky," http://en.wikipedia.org/wiki/Financial_instability_hypothesis#financial_instability_hypothesis, accessed June 11, 2012

[200] Flow of Funds Accounts of the United States 1945 to 2010 Historical Data: http://www.federalreserve.gov/releases/z1/current/data.htm, Flow of Funds Accounts of the United States current data: http://www.federalreserve.gov/releases/z1/, Data is taken from the Flow of Funds Accounts of the United States, Federal Reserve Bank and Federal Reserve Bank of New York. Commercial bank liabilities are total liabilities of the commercial banking sector, which is composed of depository institutions such as U.S.-chartered commercial banks, foreign banking offices in U.S., bank holding companies, and banks in U.S.-affiliated areas. Depository institutions such as savings Institutions, credit unions, and federal savings banks were not included nor are Investment banks (broker dealers). Shadow bank liabilities are the sum of total outstanding open market paper, total repo liabilities, net securities loaned, total GSE liabilities and pool securities, total liabilities of ABS issuers, and total shares outstanding of money market mutual funds. Data

format follows the authors' recommendations in "Shadow Banking," Staff Report no. 458, Federal Reserve Bank of New York Staff Reports, Zoltan Pozsar, Tobias Adrian, Adam Ashcraft, Hayley Boesky, available at http://www.ny.frb.org/research/staff_reports/sr458.pdf on July 2010, accessed January 12, 2012 except our graph uses annual rather than quarterly values.

[201] John Mauldin and Jonathan Tepper, *The Endgame: The End of the Debt Supercycle and How It Changes Everything*, John Wiley & Sons, 2011, pg 296

[202] The Federal Reserve Board, "Deflation: Making Sure 'It' Doesn't Happen Here," Remarks by Governor Ben S. Bernanke Before the National Economists Club, Washington, D.C., available at http://www.federalreserve.gov/BOARDDOCS/SPEECHES/2002/20021121/default.htm on November 21, 2002, accessed on June 14, 2012

[203] Wikipedia, "Devaluation," available at Devaluation, accessed on June 15, 2012

[204] Wikipedia, "Hyperinflation in the Weimar Republic," available at http://en.wikipedia.org/wiki/Hyperinflation_in_the_Weimar_Republic, accessed May 31, 2012

[205] Spiegel Online International, "Germany in the Era of Hyperinflation, Alexander Jung, available at http://www.spiegel.de/international/germany/0,1518,641758,00.html on August 14, 2012, accessed June 1, 2012

[206] Wikipedia, "Paul Volcker, available at http://en.wikipedia.org/wiki/Paul_Volcker, accessed June 7, 2012

[207] The Social Periodical, "New Weapons for the Fed to Fight Inflation," available at http://www.thesocialperiodical.com/business/new-weapons-for-the-fed-to-fight-inflation/ on February 17, 2011, accessed June 7, 2012

[208] Federal Reserve Bank of New York, "Repurchase and Reverse Repurchase Transactions," available at http://www.newyorkfed.org/aboutthefed/fedpoint/fed04.html, accessed June 8, 2012

[209] KCM Investment Advisors, Quarterly Commentary, "Over the River and Through the Wood to the Fiscal Cliff We Went...," January 2013, pg5

[210] John Mauldin and Jonathan Tepper, The Endgame: The End of the Debt Supercycle and How It Changes Everything, John Wiley & Sons, 2011, pg 12

[211] McKinsey Global Institute, "Debt and deleveraging: The global credit bubble and its economic consequences," Charles Roxburgh, Susan Lund, Tony Wimmer, Eric Amar, Charles Atkins, Ju-Hon Kwek, Richard Dobbs, James Manyika, available at http://www.mckinsey.com/Insights/MGI/Research/Financial_Mark ets/Debt_and_deleveraging_The_global_credit_bubble_Update on July 2011, accessed June 15, 2012, pgs 5, 13, 39

[212] Bridgewater Associates, "An In Depth Look at Deleveragings©," Ray Dalio, available at http://sz0121.ev.mail.comcast.net/service/home/~/Deleveraging-ray-dalio-bridgewater.2012pdf.pdf?auth=co&loc=en_US&id=215520&part=2 in February 2012, accessed April 4, 2012

[213] Ibid.

[214] Ibid.

[215] McKinsey Global Institute, "Debt and Deleveraging: Uneven progress on the path to growth," Charles Roxburgh, Susan Lund, Toos Daruvala, James Manyika, Richard Dobbs, Ramon Forn and Karen Croxson, available at http://www.mckinsey.com/Insights/MGI/Research/Financial_Mark ets/Uneven_progress_on_the_path_to_growth on January 2012, accessed June 13, 2012

[216] Bloomberg, "Stanford's Taylor: US Debt Will Explode Without Changes February 6, 2012," John B. Taylor, available at http://www.safehaven.com/article/24285/stanfords-taylor-us-debt-will-explode-without-changes on Feb 6, 2012, accessed August 22, 2012

[217] MacKay, David, "Sustainable Energy — without the hot air," Version 3.5.2, November 3, 2008, download the free copy at http://www.withouthotair.com/

[218] USA TODAY, "U.S. forecasts rising energy independence," Wendy Koch, available at http://www.usatoday.com/story/news/nation/2012/12/05/usa-energy-independence-renewable/1749073/ on December 5, 2012, accessed January 12, 2013

[219] McKinsey Global Institute, "Growth and renewal in the United States: Retooling America's economic engine," available at http://www.mckinsey.com/insights/mgi/research/productivity_com

petitiveness_and_growth/growth_and_renewal_in_the_us on February 2011, accessed August 24, 2012

[220] American Society of Civil Engineers, "Report Card for America's Infrastructure," available at http://www.infrastructurereportcard.org/, accessed September 25, 2010

[221] Black Enterprise, "5 Ways America Can Help Small Businesses Grow," Alan Hughes, available at http://www.blackenterprise.com/small-business/5-ways-america-can-help-small-businesses-grow/ on April 19, 2011, accessed August 26, 2012

[222] National Economic Council and the Small Business Administration, "MOVING AMERICA'S SMALL BUSINESSES & ENTREPRENEURS FORWARD: Creating an Economy Built to Last, Gene B. Sperling, Karen G. Mills, available at http://www.sba.gov/sites/default/files/files/small_business_report_final.pdf on May 2012, accessed August 26, 2012

[223] Wired Magazine, "How Khan Academy Is Changing the Rules of Education," Clive Thompson, available at http://www.wired.com/magazine/2011/07/ff_khan/all/ on July 15, 2011, accessed August 29, 2012

[224] Council on Foreign Relations: Renewing America, "Education Reform and U.S. Competitiveness," Interviewer: Jayshree Bajoria, available at http://www.cfr.org/education/education-reform-us-competitiveness/p25816 September 12, 2011, accessed August 26, 2012

[225] Wikipedia, "Modern Portfolio Theory," available at http://en.wikipedia.org/wiki/Modern_portfolio_theory on March 25, 2012, accessed March 27, 2012

[226] Investment Dictionary, "Investment Dictionary," available at http://www.investment-dictionary.com/ on March 27, 2012

[227] Blythe, Scott, "The Death of Modern Portfolio Theory," Canadian Investment Review, available at http://www.investmentreview.com/news/the-death-of-modern-portfolio-theory-5601 on March 11, 2011

[228] Gibson, Robert, *Asset Allocation: Balancing Financial Risk*, 4th edition, Ohio: McGraw Hill, 2008

[229] Solow, Kenneth R., and Michael Kitces, "Improving Risk-Adjusted Returns Using Market-Valuation-Based Tactical Asset Allocation Strategies," Journal of Financial Planning, 2011

[230]RIABiz, "The Yale endowment model of investing is not dead," Timothy J. Keating, available at http://www.riabiz.com/a/776012/the-yale-endowment-model-of-investing-is-not-dead on April 20, 2010, accessed September 30, 2012

[231]Trahan, Francois and Krantz, Katherine and Doll, Robert, *The Era of Uncertainty: Global Investment Strategies for Inflation, Deflation, and the Middle Ground*, Hoboken, NJ: John Wiley and Sons, 2011

[232] Ibid. pages 5-6

[233]Murphy, John J., *Intermarket Analysis: Profiting from Global Market Relationships*, Hoboken, NJ: John Wiley and Sons, 2004

[234] Kleiner Perkins Caufield & Byers, "A Basic Summary of Americas' Financial Statements," Mary Meeker, available at http://www.kpcb.com/usainc/USA_Inc.pdf on February 2011, accessed September 22, 2100

[235] Reinhart, Carmen M., and Kenneth S. Rogoff, *This Time Is Different: Eight Centuries of Financial Folly*, Princeton, NJ: Princeton University Press, 2009, pg 142

[236] Bridgewater Associates, "An In Depth Look at Deleveragings©," Ray Dalio, available at http://sz0121.ev.mail.comcast.net/service/home/~/Deleveraging-ray-dalio-bridgewater.2012pdf.pdf?auth=co&loc=en_US&id=215520&part=2 in February 2012, accessed April 4, 2012

[237] Mauldin, John. "The Lion in the Grass," *Investor's Insight*, available at http://www.mauldineconomics.com/frontlinethoughts/the-lion-in-the-grass on July 21 2012, accessed September 29, 2012